HOT
FOR
HOLLYWOOD
The life of

John E. Blakely

and the
Mancunian Film Corporation

Errata

Page ii – Photo Caption
The names James George Blakely and John E. Blakeley should be transposed.

Chapter One – Opening Paragraph.
Most people thought the Blakeley family to be Jewish and certainly their appearance gave credence to this. Although it seems likely that the Blakeley family may have had long distant Jewish lineage, James Blakely and his immediate generations were all brought up in the Church of England. Consequently, when James converted to Catholicism he did so from the Church of England faith.

Page 60.
Frank Atherton (not Bud Kelly) was the joker of the family and the one who mimicked a Mass.

Page 65 – Photo Caption
The woman pictured centre is Betty Jumel Not Joyanne Bracewell.

Addition to Filmography - Non-Blakeley Films of Interest
In 1951 a short (12min) film 'The C.W.S. (Manchester) Band was shot at Film Studios (Manchester) by the CWS Film Unit. Producer George Wynn. The band played four tunes under conductor Eric Ball.

HOORAY FOR HOLLYWOOD

The life of

John E. Blakeley

and the
Mancunian Film Corporation

-

Philip Martin Williams
& David L. Williams

-

History on your Doorstep

First published in Great Britain in 2001
By *History On Your Doorstep*,
15 Welbeck House, Brook Street East,
Ashton-under-Lyne, OL6 7TB.
Telephone 0161 308 3013.
e-mail historyonyourdoorstep@btinternet.com

ISBN 0 9518012 4 4

Printed in Great Britain by
The Book Factory
1A Mildmay Avenue
London N1 4R
Tel: 020 7354 6200
Fax: 020 7288 6944

Acknowledgements.

This book would have been impossible to write without the kind help of countless people, many of who allowed themselves to be interviewd by us. In particular, we would like to thank the following people and organisations for their help, time and patience. Mike Blakeley, Wynne and Arthur Mertz, Dorothy Stimson, Mary Waller, Members of the Blakeley Family, (including Kathleen Blakeley, Mary Blakeley, Angela Lake, Brenda Dickin, Pauline Nicholson), Ronnie Maasz, Ron Pegler, John S. Harris, Francis Searle, Eileen and Arthur Mackleston, David Alan, James Mockoski, Ruth Etchells, J.H. Moorhouse, Diane Speakman, Harold Somers, Tony Hillman, A.J. Marriot, Kenneth Cope, Jess Conrad, William Lucas, Betty Driver, Mike Harrison (Hope), The Public Records Office, Companies House, Craig Lapper & Dave Barrett at the BBFC, Eyepiece Magazine, At the BFI – John Oliver, NFTV Collections. Janet Moat, Special Collections. Maryann Gomes and Colleagues at the North West Film Archive - Manchester Metropolitan University. Manchester Central Library, Paul Eggington (BBC), Alan Howden (ex-BBC), The George Formby Society, The British Music Hall Society. We are also grateful to Ryan M. Williams who diligently read our manuscript and made corrections where necessary.

The photographs and permission to use them have also been supplied by many of the above named people to whom we are indebted. The copyright of the film stills used in this book are held with Blakeley's Films and the BBC from whom reproduction permission has been granted. Any unintentional omissions will be rectified in subsequent reprintings.

Introduction.

Like many young children during the late 1950s and early 1960s we can remember standing in the queues outside our local cinema awaiting the opening of its doors, and of the excitement that was to follow. Every Saturday morning was the same, with hardly any of our friends missing out on the cinema's children's' club. We could scarcely wait for the antics of Laurel and Hardy, George Formby, Will Hay and Our Gang (Little Rascals) all of whom were featured regularly. Then of course there were the serials, anything from the up-to-date offerings of the Children's Film Foundation to vintage Flash Gordon or Batman. Amongst all these was the occasional comic film starring some hapless fools the names of whom meant nothing to us. The stars in question were of course Frank Randle, Norman Evans and Jewel & Warriss, names that would eventually stick in our minds with more screenings of their films. Having had our first introduction to these old comics at the Saturday matinees we would endeavour whenever possible to catch them when they played on television. Although in watching these films we must obviously have glimpsed the word 'Mancunian' on the credits, the notion that the films had been made in Manchester never entered our heads.

Fast forward a few years, and with autograph book in hand we jostle with other teenagers outside the Manchester BBC television studios, in the hope of seeing various pop stars arriving for 'Top of the Pops'. Back home, proudly waving our newly acquired autographs and giving details of where we had been, Grandma casually remarked 'oh that's where they made those old Frank Randle pictures'. Of course, she was correct, those wonderful films that had given us such pleasure had been made in Manchester, and that old Church on Rusholme's Dickenson Road that housed the BBC had indeed once been the Manchester Film Studios.

Throughout adulthood, we have always kept an avid interest in film and cinema and had always been intrigued by Mancunian Films. This interest was probably heightened by the fact that there was not much information generally available. While researching for 'Flickering Memories' our 1995 book on the cinemas of Ashton-under-Lyne, our interest in Mancunian was revived. With this reawakening we promised each other that we would one day set about the task of documenting the story of John E. Blakeley and his Mancunian Films.

For we felt to have it remain untold was an injustice to a family that had been involved with the British Film Industry since its infancy.

To northern England's cinemagoers in the 1930s and 1940s, Blakeley's Mancunian Films were synonymous with slapstick comedy. His stars were home grown too, coming from the popular music halls of Lancashire and Yorkshire. With an aptitude for talent spotting, Blakeley was the first to put George Formby in to pictures. Duggie Wakefield, Sandy Powell and Norman Evans all followed from a seemingly endless production line of northern talent topped not surprisingly by the irrepressible Frank Randle.

Of course Blakely was a businessman and in realizing what his audiences wanted he also knew he didn't have to spend huge amounts of money in the films production. Nor did he go in for elaborate film techniques or in paying large amounts of money for fancy scripts. He had a unique way of making his pictures that other producers scoffed at. Yet, when he proved his films could make money others tried to follow suit. Alas, even when using similar stars and with a higher budget, they never seemed to capture the same magic that Blakeley's Mancunian films did. To view his films today one can see why critics of the day may have slammed them. But the critics' all had one failing in that they were not viewing them through the eyes of the northern mill worker or his family. With slapstick served up in large lumps the Mancunian films proved to be northern box-office successes. So much so that on occasions they out grossed London and Hollywood's more lavish and expensive offerings.

The late 1940s was a time when even the great movie moguls such as J Arthur Rank and Alexander Korda were panicking and the British film industry was in a state of collapse. Due to this, many thought that John E Blakeley was mad for opening his own film studio, especially when this studio was outside of London. In doing this, he was not only ensuring the continued production of his films but was also throwing a valuable lifeline to the many out of work film technicians at the time.

In telling the life story of John E. Blakeley we are also telling the story of Mancunian Films, a story that was to continue long after his death. During the 1960s, Mancunian went on to tap the lucrative supporting-feature market with several crime dramas after which, John's son, Tom Blakeley moved into the horror and science fiction genre.

Family portrait – Margaret and James Blakeley (seated) with James George Blakeley (standing left) and John E. Blakeley (right).

Chapter One

It seems almost certain that when James Blakeley married Margaret Quirk during the 1880s he was breaking from family upbringings. James was unquestionably from Jewish extraction while Margaret was from Irish stock, her family having settled in Ardwick during the Irish potato famine. With the Quirk's being devoutly Catholic, it appears that James converted from the Jewish faith to wed his sweetheart. The heavily populated Ardwick area of Manchester was where the couple set up home and by 1888 were living at 11, Wainright Street. The working-class populace of the district had a variety of occupations that included warehousemen, tinplate workers and labourers. In addition to these professions, the area also seemed to have had a great number of people working within varying aspects of the textile trades, including yarn dealers, fustian dealers, flannel merchants, clothiers, drapers, tailors and innumerable fent or remnant dealers. James Blakeley at this time was working as a General Broker. The happily married couple were to have two sons. James George, who was known to everyone as Jim, and John Edward, who was born on October 1st 1888. Both boys grew up in Ardwick and were educated at local schools and, due more in part to their mother, had a fairly strict upbringing within the Catholic Church.

Public Houses, Music Hall and Theatre provided entertainment for Mancunians at the end of the 19th century and the city also had regular visits from showmen and their travelling fairs. There were also sporting activities and public libraries.

Films first came to Manchester in 1896. It had been the Lumière brothers, who presented the world's first public film performance at a small Paris cafe on the evening of 28th December 1895. The small attendant audience was amazed by what they saw. With *The Arrival of a Train'* and *'Workers Leaving a Factory'*, being just an example of the selection of the short two-minute films that were screened. Britain enjoyed its first public showings of these Lumière films when Lucien Trewey showed them at London's Regent Street Polytechnic in February 1896.

To seven-year-old John Edward Blakeley, playing in the streets of Ardwick in May 1896, Manchester's first public screening of 'moving pictures' would no doubt have passed unnoticed. There is of course no

1

way of knowing if his father, James saw these films when they were screened on Monday 4th May at the St. James Theatre; or when Monsieur Trewey arrived with the Lumière's 'cinématographe' one week later at the Lesser Free Trade Hall. What is certain is that their ensuing impact would have a bearing on the future direction of the Blakeley family business.

Almost instantly, the travelling showmen had seen the financial rewards of being able to present this 'new novelty' to the public. The St. James Theatre and the Lesser Free Trade Hall were both to become the unofficial headquarters for the showmen for the next few years. The Free Trade Hall attracted many Mancunians during 1898, when it presented the first ever film of a heavyweight boxing championship. As the fight saw British-born boxer Bob Fitzsimmons defeat James 'Gentleman Jim' Corbett, a fair sized crowd would no doubt have been present. As the century turned, both venues were still attracting exceptional patronage with their regular showings, especially when offering half-price tickets and twice daily programmes. The travelling showmen also introduced this 'wonder of the age' as a fairground attraction. These shows were especially popular with the working-classes, as most towns of the Northwest held an annual 'wakes week' fair. The music halls of the area also began to use film as an added draw. Initially however, the films were used to close their shows, giving time for the stagehands to remove the sets. This coupled with the fact that the best live theatre seats are probably the worst for viewing films, meant most people took the opportunity to leave when the film flickered into life. It wasn't long however, before the films had moved to a more prominent position on the theatre bill. Another well-attended venue in city centre Manchester was Lewis's, the Market Street departmental store. They had begun to show films as part of their popular 'Penny Concerts', where films like *The Brides First Night* (1898) were shown. It actually took quite a while before it was realised that the best situation in which to view a film was in a place used solely for that purpose. Yet, we will probably never know with any degree of accuracy, which was Manchester's first permanent picture show. One of the leading contenders though, has to be one that took place in the basement of what was once 'The Musee of Mirth', on Market Street. In later years, the Market Street Picture House was to occupy this same site. It is no wonder that it was mainly the working-classes that frequented these places. For at this venue the audience had to stand on a sloping floor, making sure they didn't topple over by simply leaning on the person in front.

John Blakeley and brother Jim had both received a good education, which on leaving school enabled them to acquire substantially better employment than many other children from Ardwick's back streets. Jim was gainfully employed as an auctioneer while John found a position as a shipping clerk. By 1907, John had moved to 149 Moss Lane West, in Manchester's Moss Side district, and on 21st August married his beloved 'Bella', 19-years-old Martha Isabella Moorby at her local church, St. Wilfrid's, Hulme. At the time of the wedding, father James was describing his occupation as a draper and had for some time been conducting his business by way of market trading. Being an astute businessman however, James had also seen the rise in popularity of the bioscope films and was aware of the possibility for making money in this field.

John Edward Blakeley and his beloved 'Bella' pictured shortly after they were married.

Therefore taking both a bold step and a calculated risk, James converted empty shop premises into a picture house in Warrington town centre in 1908. In like manner, throughout the north-west, many other people were making similar conversions of small properties for the showing of films. Soon becoming known as Penny Gaffs, these usually just contained rows of wooden benches sandwiched between the screen at one end and the projector at the other. It was not everyone who saw the appearance of so many picture halls as a good thing. Indeed, there were many who thought they were, like the music halls, solely providing entertainment for the lower-classes. These people were voicing the opinion that the darkened halls of these early cinemas were putting people at risk. They believed the unsociable element amongst the population could gather there and cause any sort of trouble. This however, did not stop their rapid growth or popularity. John E Blakeley in a 1949 interview recalled their first Warrington cinema. *"It was small,"* he said. *"That cinema was only supposed to hold two hundred people, but it was such a success that six hundred were crushing in at a time"*. By his remarks it would seem he was referring to Warrington's first ever cinema which opened at 22 Golbourne Street. This cinema had a very short life and, in fact, closed during October of the same year. There is also some confusion as to the actual name of the cinema. For during research, we discovered that on one document it was named 'The Century Electric Picture Palace', but on a second, was called 'The Central'. Some years later there was indeed a 'Central Picture House' on the town's Sankey Street. It has also been suggested that James Blakeley also owned this cinema at some point before 1913. However, no firm evidence can be discovered to substantiate this. John Blakeley though, could not have been referring to this cinema when he stated that it was only supposed to hold two hundred people, as the Sankey Street cinema had been designed to hold five hundred.

It is impossible to say why that first cinema had such a short life, but by the time its doors had closed for the last time, James Blakeley had decided that the film business was now his calling. He was to return to cinema ownership but not until he had tried his hand at film renting. By 1909, from what was now the family home at 16 Union Street, Ardwick, James had begun to rent films to showmen and exhibitors. Soon he was buying around 80,000 feet of film a week, which he rented or sold; new prints from him would have cost around 6d per foot. Although already helping their father in his enterprise as trade increased, they took a decision that Jim and John should join the business full time. Consequently, Jim gave up his career as an auctioneer while John left his clerical position. During 1910, they acquired an interest in the old Arcadia Roller Skating Rink at Levenshulme, which they converted to cinema use. Shortly after this, they took ownership of numerous other cinemas in the north-west, some of which they only had a short association with. It is reputed that amongst the first of their acquisitions were the Central Hall, Salford and Picture House, Northwich.

Within the next few years, Manchester was to become the leading city in respect of picture houses per head of population. The inhabitants of Manchester totalled approximately 714,000 with 111 cinemas within its boundaries serving their needs. Keeping pace with the ever-increasing numbers of newly opening cinemas were the growing band of film renters. Manchester's film renters now included 'Ideal Film Renting', 'Bijou Film Services', 'Gaumont Film Hire', and 'Topical Film Agency'. Of course still to the fore was James Blakeley, who whilst operating from his home, had since December of 1912, been trading under the name of the 'The Central Film Agency'. Even their distribution of foreign films held no language barriers. Being silent films, it was of little importance which country they had been produced in, for all that was required for the British audience was the addition of English inter-title cards. In the years preceding the First World War over half the films shown on the British screens were of French origin. American companies were providing almost one third of the films with the rest being British productions.

By 1914 the American film product was fast gaining in popularity, as British audiences were lapping-up the comic antics of Charlie Chaplin and Flora Finch. The 'cliff-hanger' types of serial like *The Perils of Pauline* with Pearl White were also well liked. This same year had seen a good increase of business for Blakeley's Central Film Agency, necessitating in the move from home to business premises at Great Ducie Street, Manchester. The area around Victoria Street and Great Ducie Street was to become the heartland of Manchester's film industry, with almost everyone in the business, including renters and hirers and production companies, having their offices in this quarter. With their policy of buying films on the open market, the next few years were to see substantial business at the Central Film Agency. Towards the end of 1914, James Blakeley acquired the exclusive rights to a film entitled *The Abduction*, and by mid-January 1915, he had

5

disposed of all his release copies with most of the local districts having been supplied. This seemed to confirm his statement that *"the picture has gone like hot cakes"*. February saw the Central Film Agency trade showing *'The Man Who Disappeared'*, at the Central Hall, Salford. This film, produced in ten chapters by Edison, was another of the extremely popular serials. Around this time, John Blakeley could see the potential in what was the industry's first ever full-length comedy feature film, *'Tillies Punctured Romance'*. It starred Charlie Chaplin and Marie Dressler and had been made the previous year. Comedies were proving popular with audiences but most films to date comprised mostly of short one or two-reelers. Film renters, including James Blakeley, were reluctant to take a chance on this lengthy Chaplin offering. John, in looking back to this time once recalled, *"The renters all turned it down. They couldn't see it as a feature picture."* John finally convinced his father of its merits, and on behalf of 'The Central Film Agency', made the journey to London with the princely sum of £1,500 to secure the rights for Lancashire, Yorkshire and Staffordshire. John's intuition about the film was proved correct as the picture made a considerable amount of money for the Blakeley's. A report from 'The Central Film Agency' in May 1915 stated that the degree to which their open market trade had expanded was exceptional and that business was as active as ever. Throughout the year, their exclusive *'Tillies Punctured Romance'* and *'The Man Who Disappeared'* continued to register huge successes.

Having been happily married for over seven years John had become a doting father three times over. Bella had presented him with daughters Louie in 1909, Josie in 1913, and newest arrival Winifred who was born in January 1915. A more loving and caring family man, there could not have been. John was a hard working God-fearing man who would do anything and everything for his family. Joy was to be his once more when Bella announced early in 1916 that she was once more with child. With the responsibility of a growing family to look after, John now decided the time was right to venture out on his own. This decision had no doubt been prompted by the success of the Chaplin picture and the profits it had yielded, and by his knowledge of the business gained from his father. With the blessings and good wishes of his father and brother Jim, both of whom continued to run the Central Film Agency, John sought out his own offices. Consequently, in July of 1916 John E Blakeley, film renter, started his agency from offices at 54 Victoria Street, Manchester.

Three months later Martha and John were celebrating the arrival of their first son, Thomas, born on 11th October. The one dark cloud that hung over all these events was the fact that the country was in the midst of the Great War. The effect of which by 1917 was to have a bearing on the running of the two Blakeley film-renting businesses. Less than twelve months after setting up on his own, John and his brother Jim, were both serving with the military. Before joining the armed forces however, the two brothers made provision for the security of their business interests, as was the case with most young men at this time. The decision was taken therefore, to amalgamate their respective businesses into one Limited Company. Subsequently, 'John E. Blakeley Ltd' was officially incorporated on 16th April 1917 and was formed with a nominal capital of £3,000 divided into £1 shares. The directors were the three Blakeleys and one Joseph Fuller. Although the registered office of the company was originally 58 Victoria Street, just over two weeks later they changed it to 13 - 15 Great Ducie Street, Manchester. As it transpired John Blakeley was never to see action. Indeed his whole army career was to be spent with his regiment stationed at the Ardwick Barracks.

At the end of the war, both the French and British film industries had obviously taken a battering. The lack of money available for British productions during the conflict had given the upper hand to American producers, though even before the war they had begun eroding away at the French dominance of the market. There was no shortage of films to be screened during the war years and Manchester even saw several cinemas newly opened. The majority of films on offer however, were now coming from American studios. This was also affecting the film renting business, for several American studios were opening their own British rental offices for their films. It would appear that when the Blakeley brothers returned to civilian life that their business was perhaps not doing enough trade to supply enough income for the three of them; at this point Joseph Fuller disqualified himself as being a director. Consequently, while James continued to run the business of John E. Blakeley Ltd, his sons took on alternative work. Jim was to become manager of a cinema. While Seona Robertson (initial researcher at the NorthWest Film Archive) states that John was to manage the Manchester film rental office of the American 'Vitagraph' Company.

By January 1919, although all three of the Blakeleys remained as directors of 'John E Blakeley Ltd' now registered at 58 Victoria Street, the company was operating in name only. John was himself, operating independently of his family, from this same office. Jim at this time continued to work elsewhere while James severed all financial ties.

Although not being actively involved in the actual production of films, John over the years had seen at first hand the workings of many of Lancashire's small production companies, including 'The Lancashire Film Studios' which was founded by Gerald Somers in 1919 and which made several feature films including the *Romance of Annie Laurie*. (Gerald Somers several years later, as a cameraman for Universal News, was, at the request of John Blakeley, instrumental in teaching Thomas Blakeley the rudiments of camera work). There had also been the Blackburn based company of 'Mitchell and Kenyon' who had offered the faked Boer War 'Topicals'. These were actually shot on the moors around the town, yet nevertheless were to make compelling viewing. The Weisker Brothers from Liverpool were cinema owners and film renters who had also turned their hand to film production; in December of 1914, they had opened an office in Manchester. The 'Lama Film Producing Company Ltd' made several local interest films including 'Bury Mayoral Procession' made in 1913 and commissioned by the town's Art Picture Hall. By commissioning films of a local nature, the relevant cinemas could guarantee good audience attendance when they screened them. It is quite conceivable that John Blakeley, perhaps having more than a passing interest in film production, visited or even undertook some film work for one or more of these companies. 'The Manchester Film Producing Company' quite probably gave an early opportunity for John to gain experience in this field. It was established in 1916 on Rosamund Street but by 1919 had moved to being just doors away from John E. Blakeley Ltd at 64 Victoria Street. An Altrincham Cinema commissioned 'The Manchester Film Producing Company' to produce a film for them. It is believed that John E. Blakeley may have actually made the film *The Unveiling of the Chapel Street Roll of Honour*', for them.

By 1923, John had again moved offices, this time to 74 Victoria Street, in October of that year the three directors held an Extraordinary General Meeting from which a resolution was passed. This was to the effect that the company would go into voluntary liquidation, a process that was to take until 1925 to complete. John remained at the Victoria

8

Street offices as a renter under his own name, though not as a Limited Company, while Jim conducted a similar enterprise from offices at 11-15 Great Ducie Street. During September of 1925, John became a father for the fifth time when Balla gave birth to their second son, John Jnr. It was also during this year that John began a working relationship with the Leeds-based Company, Mercury Film Services Ltd. Headed by Booth Grainge, Mercury was to provide films to John until late 1926, a period which was to prove quite successful. Among the Mercury films distributed by John E. during 1925 was *'The Lost Chord'*, which had been based on Arthur Sullivan's famous song. Although made in 1917 Mercury was now putting it out and advertising it as the hit of 1925.

Since the coming of films, there had been numerous endeavors at combining sound with picture. Initially the usage of unsynchronised phonograph records achieved this and was employed with a modicum of success with musical shorts. One of the principal players in this field was the American Lee de Forest who, with his Phonofilm system, achieved a breakthrough. Between 1923 and 1927, films made at the de Forest studios were shown commercially, causing great interest. The first paying audience in Britain to see a Phonofilm was at a screening of *'Chauve Soures'* at London's Tivoli in 1925. De Forest also set up a studio at Clapham, London, where he made his first British sound-on-film productions. At this time however, the public looked upon the experiments with sound as a mere novelty. Of course, although films at this period were still silent, no one ever actually saw a film in silence. All cinemas offered some sort of accompaniment. These ranged from the large orchestras and sound effects of the plush picture palaces to the lone piano of the local fleapit. Music and song was a prime element to a series of films from Mercury Film Service and distributed by John E. Blakeley during 1925. This *'Famous Melodies'* series of four pictures, offered well-known songs from various areas of the British Isles. Like many other similar films popular at the time, this series had been made with the intention of the attendant music being provided live at the cinema. The *'Famous Melodies'* consisted of *'Songs of England'*, *'Songs of Ireland'*, *'Songs of Scotland'* and *'Songs of the British Isles'*. James A. Fitzpatrick had come to this country from America and at the request of Booth Grainge, produced all of the *'Famous Melodies'* films. Typical songs that accompanied the films included *'Just A Song at Twilight'*, *'An Old English Hunting Song'* and *Drink to Me Only With Thine Eyes'*. Clearly, where vocalisation was necessary

9

rather than just music the theatre would provide live singers to perform them. If John E. Blakeley, as the renter of these films also supplied the singers, we are uncertain; it is though, something he was to undertake in the future.

In January of 1926, Booth Grainge announced that Mercury would shortly present a sensational football feature in six reels entitled *The Ball of Fortune*. In recent years, this film has erroneously become labelled as a John E. Blakeley production. This misconception perhaps originated in 1958 when several of his obituaries stated that one of his earliest films was *The Ball of Fortune*. Perpetuated ever since in articles and student theses this has since become accepted as fact. With the world rights of *The Ball of Fortune* owned and controlled by Booth Grainge and Mercury Film Service, John E. Blakeley's connection would have been just as it was with previous Mercury films, that of distributor. Nonetheless, as a regional renter for the film John E. certainly played an important part in its eventual success. Hugh Croise directed *The Ball of Fortune*, which featured James Knight, Mabel Poulton and famous footballer Billy Meredith. Taken from a story by Sydney Horler, the plot centres on young Dick Huish (James Knight). On the death of his father, Dick is shocked to learn from his uncle (John Langley), acting as executor for the estate, that his expected inheritance is none existent. Unbeknown to Dick however, his uncle and cousin (Pat Aherne), having embezzled the money are now living the high-life. In their attempts to keep Dick and his money apart, the relatives contrive plots against him, one of which results in Dick appearing before the local Magistrate (Geoffrey B. Partridge). Befriended by Bent, his lawyer (Mark Barker), Dick avoids a gaol sentence and subsequently falls for Mary Wayne (Mabel Poulton), the magistrate's daughter. Bent is also a director of the local Stapleford Football Club, and as Dick is clearly of the athletic type introduces him to the team's trainer Billy Meredith. Coached by Meredith he manages to bring out Dick's natural talent and together they play in an important game, with Dick being the hero of the match. Meanwhile Bent having learned something of Dick's personal circumstances eventually discovers the truth about his uncle. The film of course has a happy conclusion. Not only does Dick become a footballing star; he also marries his sweetheart Mary and sees his uncle and cousin gain their comeuppance. Although the stars of the film were James Knight and Mabel Poulton, undoubtedly, a big attraction for many people was the appearance of International footballer Billy Meredith. *The Ball of*

10

Trade advertisement for The Ball of Fortune - 1926

11

Fortune' was made two years after Meredith had retired from the game at an incredible fifty years of age. To anyone even remotely interested in football the name of Billy Meredith was legendary; he was truly one of the most outstanding players of his era. His career was spent between both the Manchester clubs for whom collectively he played thirty-five years of League Football (1894 - 1924). He also played forty-eight games for his national team Wales over a twenty-five year period winning his first cap in 1895. Meredith firmly believed in players' rights and throughout his career, he held the view that they should be allowed to move from club to club. He also helped to form the players union and was once responsible for a strike as the union went into dispute with the FA. The footballing scenes featured in the film were shot at the Leeds United Elland Road ground while other location filming took place in Holbeck a suburb of Leeds. John E. Blakeley as the renter of *'The Ball of Fortune'* for Lancashire, Cheshire and North Wales, held a trade showing at the end of May 1926 at the Piccadilly Picture Theatre, Manchester. Present in the audience was Billy Meredith who was a resident within Blakeley's 'territory' and who had provided John E. with several items to help promote the film. These were later to form a window display at Blakeley's office at Victoria Street, and consisted of such articles as international caps, medals and photographs. When the film was generally available for the public to see, it was very favourably received and played to good houses across the North. At the time that *'The Ball of Fortune'* was generating business, Blakeley had also begun to promote another series of musical offerings from Mercury Services. *'Famous Song Scenas'* was a series of six pictures all directed by Hugh Croise that as *'The Famous Melody'* series had done previously all contained a selection of popular songs. The six films were *'The Veteran'*, *'Dream Faces'*, *'Shipmates'*, *'Songs my Mother Sang'*, *'Songs of the West Countree'* and *'The Irish Emigrant'*. Blakeley had arranged a trade showing for the Song Scenas in Manchester on October 27th, which again generated substantial interest from cinema booking managers. Within months Mercury were releasing yet another selection of musical films, which again Blakeley was to handle within his usual region. This collection of pictures though, was composed of a slightly different musical content; dealing as they did with the works of *'Famous Music Masters'*. Under this heading producer, James A. Fitzpatrick maintained the technique evident in his previous offerings as he dealt with the works of Bizet, Schumann, Rossini, Johann Strauss, Brahms and Edward MacDowell.

The success of Mercury's musical shorts and those issued by other companies was something of which John E. had made note. He soon began to develop the idea of forming his own company to produce similar types of films. Within the early months of 1927, while distributing such films as *'Prince in Pledge'*, *'Not for Sale'* and *'Shattered Reputations'*, Blakeley and his solicitors were finalising details, which would bring his idea into fruition. Subsequently, 'Song Films Ltd' was officially registered as a private company on February 16th with Blakeley and Charles Ogden, manager of Manchester's Piccadilly Picture Theatre, being listed as the first directors. The following month while discussions regarding Song Films direction were taking place, Blakeley held another three trade shows. These were for the films *'Strolling Players'*, *'Capture of the Rat'* and *'Valencia'*. Meanwhile it had been decided that Song Films Ltd would produce a series of one-reel operettas and an announcement to this effect was made in the trade press in April. This listed ten titles from which the first productions would be chosen. All of these would be specially adapted for use with or without vocalists and each would come with full orchestrations. John E. was soon able to provide the vocalists for this type of production should they have been required by the cinemas management. Song Films Ltd had brought in Harry B. Parkinson to direct these operettas. Hailing from Blackburn, in Lancashire, Parkinson had directed short subjects and features and was considered an ideal appointment. From what eventually was to become a series of twelve films under the title of *'Cameo Operas'*, the first four were trade shown on Tuesday 28th June. These four were *'The Bohemian Girl'*, *'Maritana'*, *'The Lily of Killarney'*, and *'Rigoletto'*. Starring in the films were members of the British National Opera Company and several of these attended and sang at the trade showing. Amongst them were Kathlyn Hilliard, Herbert Langley, and William Anderson, all of whom had lead roles. Also, present to sing on the night was the famous Lancashire tenor Frank Mullens with the Musical Director for the event being Stanley Mills. Mr Mills incidentally was the Music Director from the Manchester Piccadilly Picture Theatre. The trade show, which was presented at the London Hippodrome, was indeed a showcase of northern talent. The quartet of films had their Manchester trade showing at the Piccadilly Picture Theatre on Wednesday 13th July. Over the oncoming months the full series of twelve films was completed, all directed by Harry B. Parkinson with the exception of *'Il Trovatore'*, which had A. E. Coleby as its director. The full list of films

Trade Show Advertisement for 'Cameo Operas' - 1927

in the series were, *The Bohemian Girl*, *Lily of Killarney*, *Maritana*, *Rigoletto*, *Faust*, *Carmen*, *La Traviata*, *Daughter of the Regiment*, *Martha*, *Il Trovatore*, *The Ring*, and *Samson and Delilah*. The only surviving film from this series is *La Traviata*, a copy of which is housed at the National Film and Television Archive. Looking at the film, and bearing in mind that the film was simply a condensed ten-minute version of the well-known Verdi Opera, it appears that a great deal of thought and significant amount money had gone into its production. Nonetheless, it all works extremely well. The costumes could have graced any high budgeted drama, the locations were well chosen, and the photography was visually striking. Overall, *La Traviata* was an excellent production and was far removed from anything to be seen in Blakeley's later work. Blakeley, with the formation of Song Films Ltd, had widened his horizons from simply being a film renter, though he continued to distribute films in his own area.

The continuing development for a sound system was still ongoing in America. Successful though his Phonofilm process had been, de Forest never completely developed it. It was eventually acquired by a leading company, which in turn failed to improve it further. Tri-Ergan was a comparable system developed by a Swiss company. This also suffered similar fortune, until materialising anew at a later date. The first talking picture to establish itself as a major success was *The Jazz Singer*, starring Al Jolson. Today this film is credited as heralding in the sound era. Made by the Warner Brothers' 'Vitaphone' synchronised sound-on-disc system the film premiered in America in October 1927 and in London the following year. The huge success of *The Jazz Singer* was eventually to bring down the curtain on the silent era. In Britain, 1927 had also been a year of change. This, coming in the form of government legislation in the Cinematograph Films Act of 1927. The aim of the act was to provide some protection from the exploitative measures employed by the American studios. For quite some time, the Americans had been securing a dominance of the British screens by underhand methods. These included the practice of block booking - whereby inferior films were bundled together with the more impressive and significant films. Blind booking was a practice whereby the American products were sold even before they had been made. This new Act was now to ensure a certain percentage - or quota - of the home product had to be supplied to the British cinemas. This quota was initially set at 5% rising in yearly steps to reach a height of 20% in 1935. The 1926 production figure was increased fivefold by 1928.

Unfortunately, the new law did not stipulate a level of quality for the films - just that the amount had to be achieved. So, the British film industry was stimulated into production. Unhappily, along with the studio films of merit, there were countless others that were to become known as 'quota quickies' where the byword seemed to be quantity rather than quality.

John E Blakeley's venture into film production was to further increase with the founding of another company; Blakeley's Productions Ltd, which was registered on January 10th 1928. Before that date and during the remainder of 1927 Blakeley was indeed a busy man. He had acquired the world screen rights to Walter Howard's Melodrama *Two Little Drummer Boys*. Consequently, approaches were made to well-known producer and director G. B. Samuelson that resulted in a deal being struck between them. Samuelson was to take personal control of direction while his company Victoria Films Ltd would have control of the film throughout London and the South, along with South Wales and the Midlands. Blakeley would have similar rights for the areas of Lancashire, Yorkshire, Scotland, the four Northern Counties and Ireland. In addition, Blakeley was to have the rental rights in Lancashire and Yorkshire to six proposed films from Victoria Films. With this in mind, Blakeley planned to open an office in Yorkshire to be manned by his brother Jim. It was intended that shooting would take place at the Worton Hall studio at Isleworth, with music-hall comedian Wee Georgie Wood in one of the leading roles. John E. had also been conducting business with a French film production company that after several rounds of discussions resulted in his acquiring the United Kingdom rights to their film *Love, Man and Beast*. All the aforementioned would eventually come under the banner of the new company; Blakeley Productions Ltd that was being formulated throughout the same period. The first of John E. Blakeley's ten nation-wide trade shows for *Love, Man and Beast* was held on January 5th, 1928. The film told a dramatic tale of love, desire and excitement set in British India. With action centred on a conflict with Thugs, affrays with tigers and crocodiles and the inevitable timely rescue by British forces. Apparently, the film was *"Crammed with action, with stunts piled on stunts"*. January 5th was also the day that the trade press was announcing that *Two Little Drummer Boys* would go into production during March. Five days later, as previously stated, Blakeley Productions Ltd became an official company with capital of £100 and the first named directors being John E. Blakeley and his wife Bella. Before shooting had begun on 'Two Little Drummer Boys', Wee Georgie Wood had been appearing in Manchester and in an interview said of his impending project; "*I think it is much better to have films of the type of 'Two Little Drummer Boys' rather than the heavy German film or the conventional American stuff. If we are going to get good British films, it is much better that they are truly British in atmosphere and concerned with British people. The old melodrama ought to lend itself to a successful treatment on the films.*" Although it had been planned to shoot this film at Worton Hall when production actually started during the first week of March it was from the Southall studio. Converted from an aircraft hanger by G. B. Samuelson, Southall was the latest addition to London's studios. At the time of this production however, it had been used very little although having been opened for four years. It was to be in the 1930s before Southall was to be more active and even then without any real output of note. The story of 'Two Little Drummer Boys' has the title characters, Eric (Wee Georgie Wood) and Jack (Derrick de Marney) becoming involved in a tale of theft, deception and false accusations. The truth of the events ultimately comes out after one of the boys rescues the other from drowning. Also featured in the film were Alma Taylor, Paul Cavanagh, Walter Butler, Julie Suedo and Cameron Carr. Four to five weeks later, the shooting was completed leaving only the necessary editing to be undertaken. The finished product had its trade show in October 1928 and went on release later that year. It played at the Piccadilly, Manchester, during December as the bottom half of a double bill, being paired with 'Wait and See' starring Walter Forde. By this time what was to be the last production from Song Films Ltd had been completed. Titled 'Laughter and Tears' this again was directed by Harry B. Parkinson. The action, such as it was, involved a father and his young daughter travelling through the countryside upon a horse drawn caravan. The film reaches a climax when a nun from a nearby convent comforts the young girl after having fallen from the caravan. As in the title, laughter and tears abound when the father recognises the nun as being his long lost wife and therefore the girl's mother. As with the 'Cameo Operas', Blakeley made available full music orchestrations for the cinemas own musicians. He could also supply vocalists to accompany the film should they be required.

Two of Blakeley's singers, Betty Mullender and Hilda Bowers, came from the same Lancashire town of Ashton-under-Lyne. Betty Mullender's niece, Ruth Etchells gave us an interesting background to a singer who not only worked with Blakeley's musical films but also as a singer on later productions made at Dickenson Road. From a family of four children, two sisters Nellie and Betty formed themselves into a music-hall act, 'The Sisters Mullender'. Betty was a soprano while Nellie sang contralto and they proved quite successful in the halls of the northern towns. Later Betty left the act and pursued a solo career and around this time, she met and married Tom Street a local tenor singer of note. The couple set up home just around the corner from Hilda Bowers, whom Ruth Etchells also recalls as being one of Blakeley's quartet members. Betty and Hilda were just two of the many singers recruited by John Blakeley, which he formed into several small groups. Each quartet would be booked into a cinema along with the films. If the vocalists had to travel away from home for any length of time Blakeley also paid for their boarding house accommodation as well as their usual performance fee. The songs used to accompany *'Laughter and Tears'*, were those that seemed suitable to the content of the film and any relevant number could be used. One song in particular though, 'Ave Maria', was essential for the film, as it was 'sung' by the nun when reunited with her daughter.

On Friday November 23rd the Piccadilly Picture Theatre screened another trade show for Blakeley, on offer were a series of six short films *'Ireland - Yesterday and Today'* adapted and produced by Geoffrey Benstead. These films were advertised as 'Intimate studies of the Emerald Isle as seen through the eye of the camera' and were ideal vehicles for use with Blakeley's 'stock company' of vocalists. The topics of the films included 'Irish Personalities', 'Beauty Spots' and 'Historical Incidents'.

The year 1929 saw many of the Manchester cinemas converting to sound with only one holding out. It was to be November 1930 before the Deansgate was to open with sound. No matter what the intention of the 1927 Cinematograph Act had been, it seems that the American films were still dominating British Cinemas. Now of course, all the major studios had there own distribution offices not just in London but also in many of the major cities including Manchester. For an independent film renter like John E. Blakeley finding suitable products to supply to the cinemas was becoming increasingly difficult, especially in the wake of the American bookings systems, which were still prevalent. By 1930, he had closed his office on Victoria Street and was now operating from 48 Birch Lane, Longsight. As the silent films were fast becoming obsolete, these were easier for John E. to obtain. For a while, there were still enough suburban cinemas that had not converted to sound for him to supply with these. Producer Geoffrey Benstead had his *'Ireland - Yesterday and Today'* re-edited for release in 1931-32 as *'Come Back to Erin'*. This film along with another short series of similar films entitled *'Musical Memories'*, again distributed by Blakeley, was to help keep his stock company busy for several months. As for any production plans Blakeley may have had, the coming of sound must have undoubtedly hindered his ideas. Certainly sound had increased the cost of any new film, and even the major studios were finding the expenditure excessive. It may have been at this period however, that John E. Blakeley turned his hand to another section of the entertainment media. It appears that at some point during the late 1920s or early 1930s that John E. may well have embarked on the production of 78rpm gramophone records. It is quite conceivable that with the many vocalists he had been booking in the previous years, that he might have decided to promote one or two on record. It certainly has been claimed that he produced a number of comic records with James Baynam Dawson recording one in particular. As Mr Dawson's grandson, David Alan recalls, *"My grandfather came from the Ashton-under-Lyne area and was by trade an Entertainer & Business Affairs Caller* (stockbroker) *who dealt with the business affairs for Rochdale comic Norman Evans and musician 'Hutch'. "Grandfather was also a singer and performed comedy too and I know that he did some recording for Blakeley. For years, I used to have a copy of his record but it was unfortunately lost in a subsequent house removal".*

In 1932, the famous comedy duo of Laurel and Hardy had decided to take a holiday in Britain. Being a Lancashire lad, born in Ulverston, Stan had convinced Ollie that he would really enjoy the visit. On arrival though, it became obvious to the comedians that their trip would be no holiday. Everywhere they went hundreds of people turned out to see them. In fact, their time spent in this country continued as a whistle stop tour of personal appearances. On Tuesday August 2nd, after a visit to Blackpool, Stan and Ollie arrived in Manchester where that evening they were due to appear at the New Oxford Cinema. Relaxing during the afternoon at the Midland Hotel, the boys entertained a group of friends. Amongst these was Bert Tracey who had known the boys from the States, in particular Ollie whom he had worked with on many occasions. Before arriving in Britain however, Ollie had not seen Tracey for around three and a half years.

The two had become good friends in America meeting for the first time when they were both working at the Lubin Studios around 1914. Over the years, they had made countless films together at various studios. Tracey at one time even owned his own studio and was an efficient scenarist and director. Since coming back to Britain, Tracey had settled back in Manchester, his home city where his mother still lived, and had started to do some work with Cyril White's Rusholme Repertory Company. The Rusholme Rep was based at the Hulme Hippodrome Theatre, a building that at some point had been in the Blakeley family. Cyril White leased the building from the Blakeley's for some time before eventually purchasing it outright. It was eventually to come under the control of Jimmy Brennan. Whether at this time the theatre was still owned by Blakeley is unclear, but if so then it is entirely possible, that this is where his and Tracey's path may have first crossed. Certainly, Blakeley was present together with Tracey, that Tuesday afternoon, in the company of Stan and Ollie in their hotel room. For a short time during the get-together Stan Laurel may well have cast his thoughts back to his Lancashire childhood days as Blakeley in his broadest accent gave Ollie examples of old Lancashire dialect. Bert Tracey had his own idea for a film, which he hoped, to base upon northern life. Whether he and Blakeley had discussed this together at any point that day is unknown, but again it is quite likely. Certainly, it wasn't to be long before they would be working together.

Later in 1932, John E. Blakeley was arranging for the purchase of the King's Theatre at Longsight, Manchester. This venue along with several others belonging to the Broadhead family circuit was being put up for sale after the death of William Henry Broadhead. John E. officially took control on 30th June. It appears that at this time he also had control of the Picture Hall at Openshaw, Manchester and certainly his daughter Louisa, or 'Lu Lu' as the family knew her, was working there. John E. was eventually to sell the King's Theatre to his friend Herbert Douglas Moorhouse. It has been suggested that an informal agreement existed between them whereby if one of them purchased a property in the other's territory then they would sell it on to the other. Jack Moorhouse, nephew of Herbert, said, *"Although I have never seen this in writing, or had it confirmed, 'H D' probably did have an agreement with John E. Blakeley concerning cinemas"*.

Staff at the 'Picture Hall', Openshaw, Manchester – June 1932.
John E. Blakeley's daughter Louisa, or 'Lu Lu' is pictured centre.

With the aftermath of the 1929 US Wall Street, crash came a dramatic business collapse, which in turn caused mass unemployment and depression. In Britain, the lack of income meant many families were surviving well below subsistence level. This slump however, wasn't felt to the same degree in the Southern parts of England, where most of the workforce had been reliant on lighter industries. The depression hit hardest in the heavy industrial North of England, South Wales and Scotland where many thousands were thrown out of work. Many of the unemployed, hungry and almost penniless people would spend a couple of coppers to go to the cinema. This was not an extravagant gesture but a necessity. It was a means of avoiding the harsh weather. A place to rest after the time spent walking looking for work. A place where they could keep warm and, even if only for a short while tried to forget their problems. It was against this background that John E. Blakeley set in motion his future film production plans.

Chapter Two

Throughout his life, John E. had always had a love of the Northern music hall and its stars; in earlier days, the family had once had business interests in the Star Music Hall at Ancoats, Manchester. For many years in northern England one of the most popular acts had been 'The Wigan Nightingale,' George Formby (senior), who constantly drew great crowds especially with his comical 'John Willie' character. After his death, his son George Formby junior had taken to the halls and gradually forged a name for himself. By the early 1930s, he was appearing in reviews written by Arthur Mertz with titles like 'Formby's Good Deeds', 'Formby's Night Out' and 'Formby Seeing Life'. The reaction of the audiences to Formby had not gone unnoticed by Blakeley, who having seen some of Formby's shows dwelled on the idea of using him in a film. This practice of spotting and utilising music-hall talent was to stand him in good stead, for in the years ahead he introduced many names from the music halls to the silver screen. His initial contact with Formby came in Warrington, after seeing him perform at the Royal Court Theatre in one of his reviews. Blakeley, on meeting George and his wife Beryl, explained that although he didn't yet have a story he nonetheless knew he wanted George in a film. Formby's response, according to his biographers Seaton and Randall, was *'Ah know nuthin aboot filmin but ah'll have a bash. It's the thing to get in these days isn't it'*. The idea of breaking into films though was not new to George. For although he had so far confined his work to the stage he had, along with Arthur Mertz, just a few years earlier tried to interest a film producer in a story written by them both entitled *'Boots! Boots!'*. It wasn't long then before Blakeley and both the Formbys - for Beryl as his manager was always to the fore - had come to an arrangement and a contract was signed. George was to receive £100 per week for two weeks work plus 10% of the profits. In addition to this, it was agreed that if the film was a success, George would be guaranteed two more. Blakeley's next approach was to writer Arthur Mertz to see if he could come up with a suitable story, whereby they resurrected and duly revamped *'Boots! Boots!'*. Appointed by Blakeley, as director on the picture was fellow Mancunian Bert Tracey. John E. was severely limited in his budget having only around £3,000 to cover all aspects of the job. In May of 1933, he made a statement to the trade press saying that due to the enormous expense of making studio scenes in London, he was trying to arrange for studios in the Manchester district. *"If I succeed in getting accommodation,"* he said, *"I shall continue to make films in Manchester"*. He also added that he was hoping to gain the backing of other prominent cinema people in his plan. Although his scheme to make films in his home city was not to come to fruition until 1947, it is clear that the seed had been planted in 1933.

Unhappily, having been unable to find suitable premises in Manchester, he obviously had to turn to London. Seaton and Randall suggest that Blakeley, in seeking out low cost accommodation in London, was the one instrumental in the setting up of Albany Studios. This minor studio had been established in a small room situated above a garage on Albany Street, just off London's Regent Street. Although newly opened, it had nonetheless commenced business several weeks before Blakeley's announcement of hoping to make his film in Manchester. Nevertheless, it was to serve Blakeley's needs costing him around £30 a day, though it wasn't without its problems. With the sound stage being situated over a busy vehicle repair shop there was much banging and clamouring emanating upwards to the studio, which disturbed the 'Vistatone' sound recording equipment. A signalling system was devised and when filming began, a bell would sound in the garage and the noise ceased. George himself once remarked; *"We had to ask taxi drivers to stop their engines when we were shooting"*. Another inconvenience was the fact that the filming was taking place during a very cold October in 1933 and with very little heating in the room, the task had become a considerably arduous one.

Besides Formby, Blakeley also recruited several other music hall stalwarts. These included vocalist Tonie Forde, Scottish tenor Donald Reid and Lillian Keyes, a soprano who was also well known from her radio work. The film also featured Arthur Kingsley and introduced both Dan Young to the screen in an uncredited comic vignette, and Betty Driver – known today from her role in television's *'Coronation Street'* (see Appendix1). In *'Boots! Boots!'* George Formby played John Willie, the character created by his father. John Willie was a boot boy at the Crestonia Hotel and was in love with 'Snooky' the scullery-maid

John E. Blakeley (left) directs comedian George Formby in his first film 'Boots! Boots!'

(Beryl Formby), whom the chef of the hotel (Bert Tracey) was also pursuing. Unbeknown to 'Snooky', booked into the hotel are Mr and Mrs Clifford, her long lost Aunt and Uncle, and newlyweds Lord and Lady Royston. As the film draws to its end they all meet and when Lady Royston recognises 'Snooky' as her old school friend, Mr and Mrs Clifford realise that she is also the niece for whom they have been searching, and inform her that she is now an heiress. At this point, John Willie believing she will now no longer want him sulks off, only to be pursued by 'Snooky' for a happy ending all round. This storyline though, is all but superfluous, serving only as a link for the showing off of the various artistes and especially the talent of Formby. In this, his debut picture, George is involved in several comic sketches either solo or with other members of the cast (see Appendix 2:1) and we can see the embryo of the future Formby, the gormless simpleton. Yet, there is also the unknown, as the character of John Willie had a rather hostile and belligerent manner. One instance in the film has him uttering the lines *"You dirty double - little crosser, for two pins I'd push your face 'round the back of your neck."* Later in the scene as Beryl tries to intervene he says, *"Stand back woman or by-heaven, stand back"*, before proceeding to throw the chef through a window to off screen sounds of breaking glass. All of which is something far removed from the roles George was later to create for Basil Dean at Ealing. George's first ever screen song was *'Baby'*, sung to 'Snooky' in the hotel's boot room. Formby had a repertoire of four songs for the film, which along with *'Baby'* were, *'Why Don't Women Like Me'*, *'Sitting On the Ice In the Ice Rink'* and *'I Could Make A Good Living At That'*. It is interesting to note that the instrument he used in this film was a genuine wooden ukulele, not the banjolele he was predominantly to use later. The much-maligned Beryl Formby actually had her own moments of competence within the film too and certainly showed great expertise in performing a tap dance – which no doubt had it origins in Lancashire clog dancing. In viewing *'Boots! Boots!'* today, it is easy to see just why Formby went on to create such interest as he did within the film industry and with the public at large. We can also see for the first time the Blakeley method of filming which was to be evident throughout the rest of his career. The camerawork was in essence, kept to a minimum offering little in the way of tracking, panning, or close-ups. Obviously the constraints and limitations at the tiny Albany Studios hadn't helped in the setting up of certain shots, though any creativity Tracey as director may have had, would undoubtedly have been frowned upon by Blakeley. The result was that virtually the whole film unfolded before a static long shot camera, something that did not please the critics. This though did not distress Blakeley. He wanted a straightforward recording of music hall acts doing exactly what they did best, and in a way that his intended audience would be used to seeing them, from the theatre stalls.

The film had its trade showing on 5th February 1934 but it was more than five months later, on 30th July before it was put on release, and according to George, the film had a 'world premier' in Burslem, Stoke-on-Trent. Although he would never have said so at the time, not publicly anyway, in later life, George called it a 'lousy picture', or was he then just playing for laughs? For he went on to say *"... oh it was so dark in places you had to strike matches to see it, courting couples like it though"*. He also pointed out that the film *"packed 'em out"*. John E. in 1950 referred to *'Boot! Boots!'* as *"shocking"* adding, *"It was hissed at, at its trade show"*. The distribution of *'Boots! Boots!'* was undertaken by the London-based Butcher's Film Services who had a great success with it. At the time of the film's release, while Blakeley was travelling through Walsall he noticed the film was showing at a local cinema. Breaking his personal rule of never watching his own films, he interrupted his journey to see it. On trying to gain admittance, he was told the theatre was full and that the picture had played to packed houses throughout that week. Therefore, it seems that whatever the critics may have thought about the film, audiences in the Midlands disagreed. So too, did the people of Bristol for when the film appeared in that city one enterprising cinema manager displayed in his foyer a large array of boots and shoes; which caught the attention of the *"higher than average attendances"*.

Although Mertz and Formby jointly scripted the original story, the credits specify it as a collaboration between Cottrell and Formby. Arthur Mertz (junior) told us; *"I can't say why the credits put it down as Cottrell, but it was unquestionably co-written with my father. "Cottrell was a singer and pianist and worked with Formby. I can recall a little story about them both; I was aged about 12 or 13 and was in his dressing room one night. It may have been possibly at the Empire Sunderland. When Jack Cottrell, who was in the same show came in and said to George, 'I've just written a song that might suit you', so George handed him his ukulele and said 'you'd better sing it for me then'. So, Cottrell took the uke and began to sing Chinese Laundry Blues. So, I was in Formby's dressing room the very first time it was played to him. "As for my father's association with Blakeley, it was with 'Boots! Boots!' that he first joined Blakeley, working thereafter as a director, writer, and production manager."*

George Formby and Tonie Forde in a scene from 'Boots! Boots!'.

With the success of *'Boots! Boots!'* interest in Formby was not just coming from the public. John Maxwell, head of production at The Associated British Picture Corporation, was also taking notice. His counterpart at Associated Talking Pictures, Basil Dean, having viewed the film was also quick to realize his potential. After negotiations, Formby agreed to join Dean's company at Ealing studios, though only after the completion of a second film for Blakeley at the tiny Albany Studio.

The 11th of June 1934 was to become a landmark occasion in the career of John E Blakeley, for on this date the Mancunian Film Corporation Ltd was formed. The Mancunian Company brought together members of the Blakeley family as directors, these being John E. himself, along with his father James, wife Martha, and daughter Louisa. Two local chemical manufacturers, Arthur Shallcross senior and junior made up the board. Although registered at John E Blakeley's home address of 148 Slade Lane, Levenshulme, where they had resided for the past couple of years, it wasn't long before they took office accommodation at 54 Deansgate, Manchester. The first production made through this new company was a music- hall-based entertainment called *Love, Mirth and Melody*. Arthur Mertz had scripted what storyline it contained with direction by Bert Tracey. This film was nothing much more than a dozen or so music hall acts captured on film in the cramped confines at Albany Street. It was here where artistes such as the boy-soprano Graham Payn, The Royal Merry Four, Little Teddy Grey, Arthur Pond along with the Lionel Claff Band and Duggie Ascot's dancing girls all went through their routines.

Arthur Pond and Graham Payn were both also to appear in *'Musical Medley'* a 25-minute short produced at the same time. If this film was planned as a totally separate production or whether it was contrived from residue footage of *'Love, Mirth and Melody'* cannot be ascertained. Other stars that appeared in *'Musical Medley'* were Webster Booth, Lillian Keys and Leslie Day.

Universal trade showed *'Love, Mirth and Melody'* on Monday 13th August 1934 at their own London theatre. The following month Universal gave it several provincial trade showings including those at Birmingham, Leeds, and Newcastle. It is possible that some of these trade shows also incorporated screenings of *'Musical Medley'*, as it was certainly included on the trade programme at Newcastle. Unfortunately after these shows, the films seemed to sink without trace and apparently did not go on general release. Indeed, the British Board of Film Classification has no record at all of *'Love, Mirth and Melody'*, which makes it unlikely that they ever classified it. For private showing like trade shows a BBFC certificate would not necessarily have been required. As Craig Lapper of the BBFC said, *"It is entirely possible that the film may have been screened without a classification for the trade before being withdrawn and never released"*. Extracts from *'Love, Mirth and Melody'* were however included in *'Musical-Hall Personalities No14'* a film released in 1940. Back on surer ground, and given the success of *'Boots! Boots!'* Blakeley increased the budget for his new George Formby film *'Off the Dole'* to £8,000 and was eventually rewarded again with a box office return of around £30,000. In organising *'Off the Dole'*, John E. firmly kept his family in mind, providing for them work and the opportunity to learn aspects of the business. His father James took charge of business affairs while John E's son Tom was set to gain experience working as Assistant Cameraman. When an opportunity arose where John E. could help his family, this was something he would unhesitatingly do. When his daughter 'Lu Lu' married Frank Atherton he bought them a house, an action he was to carry out, under similar circumstances, for all his children. Son-in-law Frank Atherton was also given a position on the film working as Art Director. John E's friend and colleague Arthur L. Ward, well known in Manchester as a musician and cinema proprietor, became the film's Musical Director, and along with his band appeared in the film.

The storyline to *'Off the Dole'*, which was the first of the Blakeley films to declare itself as 'A Musical Merry Burlesque', revolved again around the character of John Willie. As a consequence of being struck off the dole, John Willie is offered a job running his uncle's detective agency, where besides tracking down and finally apprehending the bad guys, he has time to sing several songs. These include *'With My Little Ukulele in My Hand'*, *'I Promise to be Home by 9-o'clock'*, *'If You Don't Want the Goods Don't Maul 'Em'*, and *'I'm Going to Stick to My Mother'*. Formby's wife Beryl also contributed two songs. Also appearing in the film was Dan Young in his well known 'Dude Comedian' role, this early appearance also sees him performing out of character and while doing an eccentric little dance sings *'The Nearer the Bone the Sweeter the Meat'*. Having performed in music halls since the early 1920s, Young was already a seasoned performer. For a time he had partnered one of Scotland's greatest comics Tommy Lorne who became one of only a few Scots to become well known in the English Music Halls. Together, Lorne and Young made a success of *'Inside and Outside a Theatre'*, which was ideally suited to the characters they had created. Dan Young was billed everywhere as the 'Dude Comedian' always appearing as an upper-class dandy elegantly dressed in a morning suit often with top hat but always wearing a monocle and carrying a walking cane. He was a sketch comedian delivering his lines in a phoney upper-class accent. Although Dan Young was to appear in theatres throughout the country, he was always to enjoy huge success in the venues of Lancashire and Yorkshire. In the early 1940s when Jimmy Hunter took his Brighton Follies Show on tour, Dan Young's appearances helped to boost audience numbers, nowhere more so, than in Oldham where the show was to run for six weeks. Young also went on to appear many times with his own revue *'Young Ideas'* and during the forties under his own management toured with this. He was also to be constantly in demand for

Trade Show Advertisement - 1935

30

Pantomime roles and of the many performed one was the 1949/50 'Aladdin' which brought him back to Oldham's Theatre Royal to play Wishee Washee, also in the cast was Hylda Baker. After his last film for Blakeley in 1953, Young continued with his successful theatre work, touring with the revue 'Beauty on Duty' which included appearances in Liverpool, Ashton-under-Lyne and Oldham. This show toured for two years and while in Liverpool helped a young local comedian Ken Dodd on his rise to fame.

Dan Young's eccentric upper-class twit was the complete opposite of Blakeley's northern working-class characters, which is perhaps one reason why he included him in *'Boots! Boots!'* and *'Off the Dole'*, in fact Young was to become a regular for Blakeley appearing in another dozen of his films. While the official director's credit, for *'Off the Dole'* went to Arthur Mertz it is probably fair to say that John E. himself may have had a certain amount of directorial control. Arthur Mertz (junior), who was eventually to join Blakeley, recalled; *"In the main the real comedy situations would be directed by my father, Arthur Mertz senior. As to anything else, well Blakeley was always there on hand as producer, and would often no doubt direct particular scenes, but as I say Arthur Mertz did direct most of the comedy"*. With the completion of both the Formby films, it was quite evident just what it was that Blakeley wanted to capture on film and for whom it was targeted. It was no concern to him that the trade thought his productions technically inadequate. He wasn't too worried that his films would not be received well in the south of the country, for he knew the section of the public to which he was catering were those of the northern working-classes. An example of how well *'Off the Dole'* was received in the north can be seen by its popularity in the Lancashire town of Bolton where it was placed twenty-seventh out of the one hundred most popular films shown in the town for 1935. Whereas looking at its national appeal, it didn't figure at all in the top one hundred for the country and in fact, to find it one would have to go down to position five hundred and sixty-six.

For two decades, the name Mancunian Films was to become synonymous with the cinema-going public for northern-based musical comedies, an identity that remains to this day. Blakeley was to meet much adverse criticism but many that gave this simply were missing the point. In his own mind, his films achieved what he wanted them to, something, which was to be proven repeatedly by the responses of his intended audience. The Formby films had proven Blakeley's

31

instinct to be correct in that northern humour by northern comedians could successfully be transposed to film. The same working-classes that attended the music halls would also fill the cinemas to see their favourites on the screen. Blakeley travelled the north of England watching countless music-hall acts hoping to recruit the best for use in his films. This source was to provide Blakeley with almost the entire cast list for most of his films. In fact, his next film *Dodging the Dole* even read as a music hall playbill with its stars listed as follows. Roy Barbour - The Simplicity of Genius, Dan Young - The Charming Fool, Jenny Howard - The Generator of Electric Radiance along with others like Steffani's Silver Songsters and Bertini and the Blackpool Tower Band. Blakeley filmed *Dodging the Dole* at the Highbury Studios, London. According to the Kine Weekly the film had, 'Lancashire written all over it' which is just what Blakeley planned. The subject matter of the 'dole', as with his previous film, would have had strong associations for a large proportion of his intended audience. Many of who would instantly take to the antics of a work-shy pair played by Barry Barnes and Fred Walmsley. The plainly flimsy script written by Arthur Mertz revolves around the two friends thwarting Supervisor, Dan Young's attempts to find them employment. The story really does nothing, other than providing a link between a mannequin parade, cabaret show and Lancashire singsong. The India-rubber faced comic Roy Barbour also starred, excelling with a whimsical dance and funny ventriloquist routine, in which he played the dummy. Jenny Howard played the part of a flirtatious waitress to good effect giving out such songs as 'Waiting at Table'. *Dodging the Dole* had a late June trade showing before its release a few months later. Though John E. had no doubt had influenced the directing on his previous films this was the first time he had taken complete control and the first time he carried the official directors credit.

Whereas once Manchester's Victoria Street and Great Ducie Street had been the hub of the city's cinema businesses, now the vast majority had relocated to The Parsonage, an area at the rear of Deansgate. At this period, The Mancunian Film Corporation Ltd had already taken up residence here, having moved from their smaller Deansgate office. During one of Blakeley's frequent train journeys between Manchester and London, he met and spoke with Ronald Gow. It was to be a conversation that ultimately led to the story for his next film. Gow, a successful playwright, was a former pupil of Altrincham High School, to where he returned as a teacher in 1923.

It was while working there that he introduced his pupils to the medium of film, subsequently making several films at the school's summer camps. In 1929, he made a film entitled *'The Man who Changed His Mind'*, the quality of which persuaded Universal to distribute it to a wider audience. Re-titled, to his annoyance, as *'Crazy Kids'* it was screened at cinemas across the country. In the centenary year of cinema, 1996, a special plaque was erected at his former school commemorating his achievements in the use of film in education. Blakeley chatted to Gow and explained that he had an idea for his next film, which he hoped, would star Duggie Wakefield. Although having no storyline he thought the plot could centre round the popular practice of playing the football pools and perhaps could simply be titled *'The Penny Pool'*. He asked Gow if he could write a summary for him around this subject, nothing fancy just a straightforward synopsis would do. Blakeley knew that any plot Gow was to provide could be worked on and expanded by Arthur Mertz once back in Manchester. Gow did just as was asked of him and duly presented Blakeley with his outline before the train reached its terminus. Although the completed film did not fully acknowledge Ronald Gow as writer of the story, he did a few days after penning the outline receive a cheque for £20 in payment. Ronald Gow had himself written a pools orientated scenario titled *'Lancashire Luck'* which was filmed by Paramount-British in 1937. The film starring Gow's wife, Wendy Hiller, centred on the Lovejoy family's £500 football pools win. Gow eventually transformed the story into the successful play, *'Ma's Bit O' Brass'*. As Ronald Gow's son Anthony says, *"The meeting between my father and Blakeley throws up an interesting question"* That being, *"Which was written first? "I believe the story for Lancashire Luck dates from some years earlier and perhaps my father was able to re-cycle it on the train journey and would have been very pleased to receive an unlooked for payment"*. Of course, alternatively it may well have been *'The Penny Pool'* that inspired Gow to go on and write his scenario for *'Lancashire Luck'*. As Anthony Gow points out, *"all this is conjecture and I am afraid that my mother, Dame Wendy Hiller, at the age of 87 can throw no light on the matter.* Arthur Mertz still carried a credit on the film but tellingly this was only for story adaptation. Filmed at Highbury Studio, London the completed film was trade shown in June 1937 and went on release during October. It told a simple story of blossoming love between the son of a wealthy business owner and a working-class woman so nearly cheated out of her football pools winnings. There are of course the obligatory scenes of music, dance and songs. Arthur Mertz and Albert Stanbury, another Manchester man, hailing from

Urmston, had jointly written the special lyrics. Their sentimental *'How Sorry I Am For Old People'* and *'Lancashire'* with its words of northern patriotism - *"what Lancashire does today all England does tomorrow"* - were obviously well received. Though, it was the comic slapstick element that supplied the highlights of the film. Star of *'The Penny Pool'* was Yorkshire born comedian Duggie Wakefield, who along with his 'gang', Billy Nelson, Jack Butler and Chuck O'Neil became very popular during the 1930s performing in Archie Pitt produced reviews. They also appeared in the Royal Command Performance at the London Palladium in 1931. The gormless buck-toothed Wakefield with an hair style from 'Our Gang's' Alfalfa school of hairdressing, slicked-down and centre parted, was no newcomer to the world of films having already appeared with his sister-in-law Gracie Fields in two of her pictures *'This Week of Grace'* and *'Look up and Laugh'*. In *'The Penny Pool'*, Duggie and his gang perform several knockabout routines including one in a brass band, his famous garage sketch and a grand finale where he and great friend Billy Nelson drag up. The garage sketch was one performed regularly in his stage act. Working as motor mechanics, and after some knockabout with tyres, the gang would set about fitting and inflating an inner tube. Inevitably, they would put so much air into it that the inner tube soon resembled one from a tractor rather than a car, and so enormous did it eventually get that it finally exploded. On stage, the sketch was always presented using India Tyres and the company, in a form of early sponsorship, even financed the performance. Whether Blakeley had any similar arrangements with India is not known, but in the film, several India Tyre advertisements can be seen, especially during the tyre inflation scene. The director's credit on this film went to George Black junior, as too did Blakeley's next production *'Calling all Crooks'*. Again written by Arthur Mertz the story for *'Calling All Crooks'* is that of a con man Devane, played by Leslie Perrin and his attempt to obtain money from Dentist Dr. Bellamy. Suspecting Devane's wrongdoing, the dentist's daughter Joan, played by Helen Barnes, engages a detective agency to help prove her notion. In the roles of the investigators are the film's stars Duggie Wakefield and his gang, Billy Nelson, Chuck O'Neil and Jack Butler. Coupled with their unique style of detective work and after having the suspect under surveillance they soon confirm Joan's suspicions. All ends well though, as Devane is apprehended and Duggie himself wins the love of a delighted Joan. Duggie and the Boys throughout the film deliver a string of hoary old gags, though apparently nonetheless funny for being resurrected. They also inject a

Yorkshire comedian Duggie Wakefield star of Mancunian Films' 'The Penny Pool' and 'Calling all Crooks'

35

good measure of slapstick into the proceedings including a comical whitewashing scene, an appearance by a pantomime type cow and a knockabout routine in the dentist's surgery. Adding to this 'merry musical burlesque' as Blakeley now subtitled all his films, were a host of music hall acts given the opportunity to go through some of their routines. These included a ventriloquist, acrobatic dancers and several singers. According to the Kine Weekly after the film's June trade show, 'Laughter was seldom absent from the screen; and was good fun for those who did not take their pleasures too seriously'. As a guide to cinema owners and booking managers, the Kine Weekly described it as being a *"cast-iron two-feature programme booking for the masses; particularly those in northern areas"*. This of course was exactly the audience for whom Blakeley had made it. The film went on general release during October 1938.

At this time, many music hall and revue artistes were making appearances in a series of short films produced by newsreel company 'Pathé Gazette'. These films were always exhibited in support of the main feature and were well received. Such an astute businessman was Blakeley that though his films had already earned him profit; he nevertheless managed to squeeze more out of them. Emulating Pathé's policy, he began in 1938 to release a series of short films *'Music-Hall Personalities'* which consisted of songs, dances, and comic routines taken from his back catalogue of films. Blakeley was also shrewd enough to release the Formby material separately and *'Music-Hall Personalities 2,4, & 6'* were issued simply as *'George Formby'*.

With the declaration of war in September 1939, what in retrospect has been termed the phoney war period began, and with it Britain's entertainment industry ground to a halt. The government in its infinite wisdom felt that the congregating of people in the country's theatres and cinemas would be too much of a risk in case of German air-raids. Consequently, all live venues and picture houses closed their doors leaving the public with their sole entertainment coming from the radio. On the film production side many studios were appropriated and put to use for the storage of munitions and other war materials. With no air-attacks materialising however, and with mounting pressure being put on them, the government relented and allowed places of entertainment to reopen.

On the family front parents across the country, fearing for the safety of their children began evacuating them to quieter rural areas. In this respect, John Blakeley was like any other parent or grandparent, in that, to him his family meant all. Consequently, having acquired suitable property, he sent most of his family — grandchildren included — off to the peaceful seaside town of Cleveleys. It was here that his son-in-law Bernard Kelly was stationed with the RAF, and where his wife Winifred gave birth to their second child, Brenda. From time to

John E. with two of his grandchildren in the safe wartime haven of Cleveleys.

time, several members of the family would return home to check on their respective houses, but Cleveleys was to be a safe haven for some time under John E's watchful eye.

The government found that in the medium of film they had at their fingertips a very powerful tool. Films were enormously popular with the masses and the authorities could easily manipulate them to impart propaganda and information - through newsreels, documentary and official Ministry of Information Films. It was in dispensing its escapist and morale boosting entertainment however, that the cinema excelled, taking the peoples minds away from their day-to-day wartime routines.
 Now, more than ever, audiences wanted to laugh when they went to the pictures and they wanted to avoid, even if only for an hour or so, their austere surroundings and the trappings of a country at war. Several film producers were quick to meet these requirements and music-hall stalwart Arthur Lucan, alias Old Mother Riley was the first comic to hit war-time cinema screens in the Butcher's release of *'Old*

Mother Riley Joins Up', the same company also released *'All at Sea'* starring Sandy Powell. Both films had northern comics as their stars and it wasn't long before the big guns were rolling out their own northern talent, Gracie Fields in *'Shipyard Sally'* and George Formby in, perhaps his best outing, *'Let George Do It'*. In 1940, after a break in production at the onset of the war, Blakeley struck a deal with London based Butcher's Film Services, which resulted in them helping to finance and distribute his latest offering *'Somewhere in England'*. As previously stated the planning of all of Blakeley's productions took place in Manchester. The Mancunian offices situated at 3 The Parsonage would at this time have been a hectic place and from his own third floor office, Blakeley took sole charge of much of the arrangements. There was the matter of the cast, for Blakeley always knew who he wanted to appear in his films. He also took personal control when it came to negotiating terms with them, with all the necessary contracts being drawn up within the confines of his office. For *'Somewhere in England'*, Blakeley was to bring together for the first time two well-known and popular northern comics', Harry Korris and Frank Randle. There was also the problem of finding and hiring a suitable London studio and cinematographer to be resolved. Space and time was eventually booked however, at the Walton-on-Thames studio. Situated among suburban residential houses, Walton was another of the small independent studios. Although none of these small studios offered anything like the expertise of Pinewood, Elstree or Shepperton, they did nonetheless provide rudimentary facilities and many were quite friendly places to work. Walton itself, however, was perhaps one the worst of these second-rate studios. For a cinematographer, Blakeley signed-up Geoffrey Faithfull a man of vast experience, and as it turned out a man who was to work for him on a further four occasions. Another third floor office at the Parsonage was regularly occupied by the mysterious scriptwriters Roney Parsons and Anthony Toner. Mysterious in the fact that none of them actually existed; they were in reality pseudonyms respectively of Arthur Mertz and John E. Blakeley. Mertz was also to collaborate again with talented lyricist Albert Stanbury both of whom were responsible for the film's catchy songs and rousing patriotic finale.

Comedian Harry Korris had become a firm favourite with the northern audiences through his leading role with the Arcadian Follies. For over a decade he had starred at Blackpool's South Pier entertaining the holiday crowds, while at Christmas he would be cast

38

in pantomime. He was soon to gain national fame with the success of the stage and radio show *'Happidrome'* which was broadcast by the BBC for seven years. A film version was also released in 1943, which incidentally also had Geoffrey Faithfull as cinematographer. One of Korris's *'Happidrome'* co-stars was Robbie Vincent who played the character of 'Enoch' in the show, the same persona in fact that he portrayed in *'Somewhere in England'*. Randle's appearance in this film was to set in motion a long association between him and Blakeley. Randle, born Arthur MacEvoy in Wigan, Lancashire, was a boyhood friend of George Formby. His early show business career started in Blackpool when he became part of an acrobatic troupe before going solo as a comedian with his own touring company *'Randle's Scandals'*. A member of his company was his friend and drag artiste Gus Aubrey who was also to appear in several Blakeley productions. Randle was an eccentric northern comic whose Lancashire dialect and earthiness didn't travel well south of Birmingham. He wasn't a comedian in the sense of the stand-up variety but involved himself instead in sketches and monologues. His small collection of standard gags lasted him his whole career. Audiences became so used to these that they almost became identifiable as catch phrases. Examples of which include *'Gerroff mi foot'*, *'I've supped some ale toneet'*, and *She's a hottun'*, a 'hottun' being a Randle-ism for any young shapely female. Randle created several characters his most famous being the toothless octogenarian 'Old Hiker'. Dressed like an overgrown Boy Scout in khaki shorts, with legs like two knotted pieces of string. With beer bottle in hand he would, in-between belches, regale his audience of his various escapades. *"...Ah found a girl to goo owt wi' mi, an we went for a walk in t'country. Ah said, a penny for thi thoughts, and she clapped mi reight across mi lughole. I said what's up wi thee, I only said a penny for thi thoughts. Oh, she said, I thought you said a penny for my shorts".* Two other similarly aged gents were 'The Old Boatman' from his sketch 'Any more for Sailing' and 'Grandad' from 'Grandpa's Birthday'. Much of Randle's humour was based on him either playing a drunkard, a lecher, a character of unruly and violent temperament, or one who held a great disdain for authority. More often than not, it was all of these rolled into one. Randle had his critics, most of which thought him to be rude, crude and filthy. He himself however, was often quoted as saying, *"I'm vulgar but not filthy"*. Many a southern audience couldn't see the difference nor for that matter could the office of the Lord Chamberlain, which on several occasions censored his shows, but this said northern audiences loved him. To these northerners, Randle was one of their own sort.

Randle as the eccentric 'Old Hiker'. The character also made a film appearance in 'Somewhere in England'.

He was the next-door neighbour, the workmate, the pal from the pub - full of ale and drunken staggers. Randle and the characters he portrayed lived in every northern town. Almost every back-to-back terrace house, with its communal yard and loo, had a Randle. This was their life; they didn't shy away from it because everyone they knew was the same. Perhaps the only time they may have felt ill at ease was during 'wakes week'; the one occasion they may have managed to get away from home to the 'workers' resort of Blackpool. Then perhaps, while in the confines of a guesthouse, would they be on their best behaviour. So, to see a larger than life Randle on a Blackpool stage it was no wonder they laughed, they knew exactly where he was coming from, and he knew them, all of them. Indeed much the same could have been said of Blakeley, in the sense that he too knew the people. He was one of them. He knew their lifestyles, their needs, hopes, and most importantly their funny bones. He knew what made them laugh and who made them laugh. Randle as one of the most popular stars in northern theatres was one of these people and indeed was why Blakeley had signed him up for a film. The thin storyline of 'Somewhere in England' sees Korris cast as the typical stereotype of army sergeants, with Randle as one of his new recruits. The pair aided by Dan Young and Robbie Vincent come to the aid of a young soldier, falsely accused of theft by a rival in pursuit of the adjutant's daughter's affections. As the film develops, the sergeant is continually on the receiving end of Randle's comic shenanigans and his complete disregard for army life. The inevitable cabaret scene of the film features Randle performing one of his famous stage characterisations the 'old hiker'. Undoubtedly the completed 'Somewhere in England' was a great hit with working-class audiences throughout the north. It also became popular with servicemen, for again in Randle they could see themselves. How often they must have wanted to handle their superior officers in the way he did. Poking fun, at the sergeant and in fact at the whole establishment, was something they could never have dared to do. Arthur Mertz Jnr. son of Blakeley's screenwriting partner was at this time serving with the army in Iceland. Recalling the time he said, *"I can recollect a time when the sergeant in charge of the ENSA film unit came to me one day and said 'there's a ship waiting for the ice to break and when it gets through its got a film aboard which will interest you'. "When I enquired as to what it was, I was really surprised to find out it was 'Somewhere in England' the film my dad had helped with. "Well, the projector was fixed up in the mess and there was food laid on and of course a bar. "We only had the one projector so when one reel ended another had to be put on and laced up. "Of course while this was happening the*

41

bar was open and everyone was getting another drink. This was a routine, which went on until the film had reached its end, by which time a considerable amount of booze had been consumed. "I was with the West Riding Division which was full of north countrymen. So there we were watching these northern comics, Randle, Korris, and Robbie Vincent with all their gags about 'Yates' Wine Lodge', drinking beer and other typical northern delights, which went down enormously well with the men. "So much so in fact, that the film was shown four times during that night". The public's reaction to 'Somewhere in England' and in particular to Randle's performance prompted Blakeley to come up with more of the same.

This success was to cement Blakeley's production relationship with Butcher's, which was now to last until the opening of his own Manchester studio. Soon audiences were taking to army life Blakeley style as he recruited the same team who had appeared in the 'England' success for a follow-up, 'Somewhere in Camp'. This winning formula eventually was to lead to a third production 'Somewhere on Leave'. The filming of 'Somewhere in Camp' commenced late in 1941 at the Riverside Studio with Stephen Dade as cinematographer. Dade would later become remembered for his work on the epic film 'Zulu'. Geoff Faithfull would be back as cinematographer the following year when 'Somewhere on Leave' went into production at the same studio. The war years had seen little action at the two-stage Riverside Studio with filmmakers under using it. Originally opening in 1935 the owners had by 1937 gone into liquidation. By the time Blakeley was shooting there, British actor Jack Buchanan had taken over the premises. Although the likes of Randle and Korris were the stars of the 'Somewhere' films; they actually had little involvement with any of the Toner and Parsons scripted plots. This was left instead to a cast of straight actors who, adequately if somewhat tediously, carried the scenarios. These simple storylines were in effect incidental; they were just the hooks on which the various comic routines could be placed. Audiences didn't go to watch the stories unfold they went to see their music hall favourites. As the star of 'Somewhere in Camp', only Randle could have made an entrance as he did. After bursting out through the canteen doors with legs wobbling and hips suggestively thrusting forward, he loudly belched before uttering his first words, *"Eh! I'm full o'gas".* Joining his fellow recruits on the parade ground, he soon showed his violent streak and in a set-to with Dan Young, threatened, *"I'll knock yer stomach from yer chest". "I'll separate yer from yer breath".*

His contempt for authority soon surfaced when an officer came to inspect the squad.

Officer: *Now my man what were you in civilian life?*
Randle: *Who me?*
Officer: *Yes you.*
Randle: *Oh you mean when I was working for a living.*
Officer: *Yes when you were working.*
Randle: *Oh I used to train performing fleas.*
Officer: *Performing fleas. You had to scratch for a living eh.*
Randle: *Don't be a twerp.*
Officer: *I beg your pardon.*
Randle: *Oh I'm sorry Sir... Have you ever seen a performing flea?*
Officer: *No.*
Randle: *Lend me a flea will you? Do you know it took me three months to train two performing fleas to do the splits on a circular saw?*
Officer: *Oh, well no wonder you look tired. Where do you come from?*
Randle: *You're damned inquisitive aren't you?*
Officer: *Do you know who you are...[talking to]?*
Randle: *I beg your pardon Sir. As a matter of fact the stork brought me.*
Korris: *Well tell the stork to take you back.*
Randle: *You shut your gob.*
Officer: *(to Korris) Yes, you be quiet.*
Randle: *(to officer) I'll tell him, I'll tell him.*
Officer: *Do you know that you are talking...[to an officer].*
Randle: *I. I do beg your pardon Sir. As a matter of fact where do you come from?*
Officer: *If you must know I come from Cowes.*
Randle: *Hmm... Blimey you look like it too.*
Korris: *Silence. Do you know who you are talking to?*
Randle: *I'm talking to the engineer not the oil rag.*

An example of Randle's drunken lechery can be seen in *'Somewhere on Leave'*. In one incident he is seen sitting close to a Land Girl, to whom he makes his advances; *"By gum I'll bet you're a hot 'un... "...You seem a grand bit of stuff"*. Trying to give him the brush off she says, *"I wouldn't call shyness one of your drawbacks"*. *"Not likely*, says Randle, *...if you want anything in this world, you've got to grab it... Give us a kiss"*. *"Go on give us a kiss there's nobody looking"*. He then lunges forward in his attempt to hold her in an embrace. Alcohol comes to her rescue however, in the form of a tray of cocktail apéritifs.

The Third in the 'Somewhere' series saw the gang 'On Leave'

The drinks' waiter having first proffered one to the lady then offers one to Randle. Without hesitation, Randle's response is *"Aye, I might as well. By gum they're little 'uns aren't they"*. Picking up the small cocktail, he quickly drinks it, adding, *"Good health"*. Placing the empty glass on the tray, he picks up another full one, and while holding it quips, *"You'd better bring um in pint pots next time"*. He then takes up one more to drink. Exchanging the now empty glass for yet another full one, he adds, *"I'll have that as a chaser, I never leave owt if I can help it. Good health"*. *"Fetch some more won't you"*. Wherever Randle was working, be it on stage or film set, his dressing room always had to be supplied with what he termed the essentials. His 'essentials' of course came in a bottle. More often than not, his dressing room was stocked with crates of Guinness and a few odd bottles of spirits. It wasn't a matter of them being there for a sociable drink after a performance for Randle could drink at anytime. On many occasions, he would have a bottle of Guinness and a Woodbine for breakfast and by the end of his day, his alcoholic consumption could be immeasurable.

Both *'Somewhere in Camp'* and *'Somewhere on Leave'* continued the now customary musical concert type sequences. In these films, they were featured as army camp concerts in which Randle and Korris appeared in different guises. In *'Somewhere in Camp'* Randle and Korris perform a sketch 'Wanted a Housekeeper'. Korris in drag is the target for Randle's lecherous 'Old Man' (see Appendix 2:2). The same situation also faced Dan Young when he dragged-up for the sketch 'Putting up the Bans' which featured in *'Somewhere on Leave'*. Both these short sketches gave an idea as to what Randle's characters on stage were like, although here it was sanitised to avoid the film censor. Just how successful the 'Somewhere' films had been during the war years was proven by Julian Poole from Manchester Polytechnic. For while undertaking research, he came across the attendance figures for a Macclesfield cinema. These figures clearly show *'Somewhere in England'* as the fifth most successful film screened there in 1940. When they showed *'Somewhere in Camp'* it attracted audiences in enough numbers to place it second to *'Mrs. Miniver'* the country's top grossing film of 1942. In 1943 Blakeley's *'Somewhere on Leave'* was again to come second this time to the American *'Holiday Inn'*. Although these figures only refer to the one cinema, they can be taken as an indication to the drawing power that the films had in the north of England.

Part of the deal with Butcher's allowed Mancunian Films to distribute the films in Lancashire, Cheshire and North Wales, while Butcher's held rights for the rest of the country. Mary Waller (nee Smart) who was eventually to become John E. Blakeley's private secretary remembers this period well. *"I started work at the Parsonage as a junior clerk in 1943 and I soon found out that there was more to a film than seeing it at the cinema. The office was a hive of industry with the release of the latest film 'Somewhere on Leave'. All the arrangements for its distribution had to be organised and the film renting of his previous films was still ongoing. John Blakeley was a very generous person to those who were loyal to him. However, he worked extremely hard and expected his staff to do the same."* To say he

John E. travelled the region as his own Representative for Mancunian Films.

worked hard was a bit of an understatement, for there were not many people in the industry that would have been prepared to undertake what Blakeley did. For after all his pre-production planning and the actual filming, Blakeley took on the role of company representative. There were separate reps for Cheshire, Liverpool/North Wales, while Blakeley himself set off on the roads of Lancashire trying to sell his finished products to the cinemas of the region. Mary Waller and the company's other clerks from their first floor offices would confirm all bookings made by the reps. They would then have to estimate the takings of each cinema and from this pay a percentage to the rep. Once the cinemas had actually screened the film, they would send into Mancunian a 'returns form' showing their actual takings. From this, the clerks would work out just what they owed to Mancunian, which they then charged out to the cinemas. They would also pay any balance owed to the reps at this time. Butcher's Films in London would have had their own stock of films for distribution to the rest of the country. Mancunian's copies were stored, along with all Blakeley's other films in their vaults on the top floor of the Parsonage building. Each week it would be part of the clerks' duties to type out from a logbook just which films were to be sent out. These were then sent down to the basement where they would be collected for distribution by F.T.S (Film Transport Services). Everyone at the Parsonage would start the same routine over again when Blakeley started on his next production during 1943. Locked away in their third floor office John E. and Arthur Mertz again took up their alias's to pen the screenplay for *'Demobbed'*. As the war had not yet come to its end, the cinema-going public was still looking for pictures to make them laugh. Unlike the *'Somewhere'*, films *'Demobbed'* had no Korris or Randle. In fact, Randle in 1943 had appeared in the T.A. Welsh produced picture *'Somewhere in Civvies'* which people often mistake for being a Blakeley/Mancunian Production. For *'Demobbed'*, Blakeley turned to the talents of Norman Evans, Nat Jackley, regular Dan Young and Tony Dalton. Norman Evans was a music hall sketch comedian, noted and still fondly remembered today for his *'Over the Garden Wall'* sketch. Dressed in drag Evans became 'Fanny Fairbottom' a middle-aged working class housewife of ample proportions. Wearing a wig and mobcap Evans looked every bit the typical northern wife, gossiping to her neighbour over the garden wall. Norman Evans had entered show business through the amateur dramatic society in his hometown of Rochdale. In his spare time, he took every opportunity to appear on stage. In 1931, he was in a fund raising show for the town's football club. Top of the bill, Rochdale's own Gracie Fields, suggested he should turn professional. Three years later Norman decided to take the plunge when Oswald Stoll saw his act and presented him with a contract. Three more years saw Norman appearing on the first of his three Royal Command Performances. Both his radio show 'Good Evans' and the touring show *'Over the Garden Wall'* proved hugely successful. They also brought to the fore a young lady named Betty Jumel who was to play an integral part in both. Betty, also to appear in *'Demobbed'*, was short on stature but big on laughs. Her bubbly and bouncy personality made her a firm favourite with audiences especially in pantomime. She was one of the few females to successfully play Dame. Betty Jumel's versatility stood her in good stead, as she was equally at home singing, dancing or as a comedienne. Also co-starring in *'Demobbed'* was Nat Jackley whose career had started as a clog dancer with the Eight Lancashire Lads before evolving into a much loved sketch comedian. Billed as 'Rubber

Neck' due to his Giraffe-like neck, a feature he became renowned for, the tall and lanky Jackley would project his head forward giving the idea that his neck was even longer. This had audiences in fits of laughter before he'd even spoken a word. Adding to this was Jackley's eccentric walk that gave the impression his legs were made of rubber. The first time we see the four stars in the film is when they are at the demobilisation office. This scene is centred on Jackley's exaggerated walk which itself leads into a sort of dance routine involving the crazy quartet. To accentuate Jackley's gangling appearance he is dressed in an uncommonly short kilt, tight tunic and a tall bearskin cap. His whole appearance is made to look even more absurd by being partnered with the diminutive Tony

The Versatile Betty Jumel

Dalton. Before obtaining their discharge papers there is time for more of the army-type of humour, made popular in the 'Somewhere' films and still a favourite with servicemen, where the motley privates' cheek their sergeant.

Sgt:	*Now mi lad what were you before you joined the army?*
Pvt Dalton:	*I was a fitter sir.*
Sgt:	*A fitter?*
Dalton:	*Aye, every time I was put on a draft I had a fit.*
Sgt:	*Just remember who you're talking to. Do you see these stripes? How d'you think I earned those?*

Dalton:	*Through creepin'.*
Sgt:	*I'll creep you! Tell mi, mi lad what made you join the army in the first place?*
Dalton:	*I joined the army for three reasons.*
Sgt:	*Three reasons?*
Dalton:	*Aye.*
Sgt:	*What were they?*
Dalton	*First of all I was patriotic.*
Sgt:	*Yes.*
Dalton:	*And then I wanted to fight the enemy.*
Sgt:	*And the third reason?*
Dalton:	*Well two fellas came and fetched me.*
Sgt:	(To Private Evans) *What's your name?*
Evans:	*Evans.*
Sgt:	*Good Evans.*
Evans;	*No, just Evans. E for Expert. V for Victory. A for 'andsome. N for Noble.*
Sgt:	*And S for scrounger. And I suppose you've also been in Africa?*
Evans:	*Oh Aye. I was in Tunisia when t'first shot were fired.*
Sgt:	*Were you really.*
Evans:	*And by the time they'd fired again I was back in Rochdale.*
Sgt:	*Tell me did you have any status when you were abroad?*
Evans:	*Come again.*
Sgt:	*Rank! Rank!*
Evans:	*Aye you do hum a bit.*

After being demobbed, they next visit the Labour Exchange where a knock-about routine with an umbrella is played out. Here they are offered a job in the packing department at James Bentley, Scientific Instrument Manufacturers. Sitting idly about on their first day with no interest in starting their new labours, they are approached by James Bentley's son, John (Neville Mapp).

Bentley:	*Are you the new men just started?*
Jackley:	*We're the new men all right but we haven't started.*
Bentley:	*Why not?*
Jackley:	*We're on strike.*
Bentley:	*On strike, before you start?*
Jackley:	*You've got it mate.*
Bentley:	*That's impossible. Please stand up and tell me all about it.*
Evans:	*Oh no, this is a sit-down strike.*

49

Bentley:	*But this firm's a hundred years old and never had a strike.*
Jackley:	*Well its time they had one.*
Bentley:	*What are you striking for?*
Young:	*Well we er... haven't decided yet.*
Evans:	(To Young) *Isn't it for more wages?*
Young:	*That's it. More wages and shorter hours.*
Bentley:	*Shorter hours. But this firm is known to work shorter hours than most - what do you want?*
Evans:	*Well how many minutes are there in an hour?*
Bentley:	*Sixty of course.*

All three take a sharp intake of breath at the shock of this.

Evans:	*That's too long... Oh, thirty minutes is plenty long enough.*

At this statement, the pals all raise their hats and cheer.

Bentley:	*Well this strike is unofficial surely. Are you members of the union?*
Evans:	*Aye we are an' all.*
Bentley:	*Which union?*
Jackley:	*Our own we formed it this morning.*

John Bentley is romantically pursuing Norma Dean, secretary to Mr Black, the works' manager. Although Norma is interested in John, things are not straightforward as Black himself has also taken a liking to Miss Dean. Norma doesn't appreciate Black's attentions as she suspects he is stealing from the firm. Enlisting the help of Evans and Co. they eventually prove that Black has been selling company property to help pay off his gambling debts. As usual, there is the indispensable variety show, which is given under the guise of a celebration of the company's centenary. Featured were the light opera singers Webster Booth and Anne Ziegler who presented another Blakeley staple, a Song Scena; titled 'The Garden of Romance' in which the duettists sang a medley of romantic songs. Nat Jackley, Dan Young and Betty Jumel appeared in a sketch entitled 'The Human Dummy', in which Young pretended to be a ventriloquist with Jackley as his dummy so that they could cheaply share the same hotel room (see Appendix 2:3). Norman Evans gave an interpretation of his *'Over the Garden Wall'* skit. Felix Mendelssohn and his Hawaiian Serenaders also gave a musical offering in a fund raising cabaret dance, which featured later. To their music Jackley, Young and Jumel present a knockabout Hawaiian dance routine, while Evans in glamorous drag conducts the orchestra. The film ends with the foursome being made company directors their reward for exposing Black. At a cost of just over £30,000, *'Demobbed'* was shot at Riverside Studio by cinematographers Geoff Faithfull and G. Gibbs. The completed film was trade shown in February 1944 and by 1946 had been screened in half the country's cinemas with estimations that it would earn three times its production costs.

Dan Young (Left) and Norman Evans flank Nat Jackley
in a scene from 'Demobbed' - 1944

Chapter Three

As the war with Germany ended, Blakeley and his Mancunian production team were ready to put Frank Randle into his first peacetime film. Though there would be a short pause while they waited for space at Riverside; for, although the financial backing from Butchers was helping with the increasing studio fees it couldn't guarantee finding studio space at the right time.

The British public had just come through six years of hostilities and what lay ahead now was the determined desire to return to a normal existence. This was however; to be no easy task, for many people the war had changed their lives drastically. A new kind of comradeship had developed between people from all types of backgrounds. Side by side had stood the road-sweeper and the bank clerk, the labourer and the businessman. On the home front, another social upheaval had seen the women taking on different roles, as together they filled the positions vacated by the fighting men folk and this role reversal was also to break down many barriers. These then were some of the social changes that Blakeley tried to encapsulate in his first post-war feature *'Home Sweet Home'*. Previously many of Blakeley's film titles had been chosen to typify a period and this new film was no different, adopted it appears, to reflect a country now at peace and the feelings of those returning from overseas. Another aspect of role reversal was evident from the opening scene of *'Home, Sweet Home'*, where; with his pregnant wife in bed Randle is depicted running the household in typical 'housewife' fashion. He is seen looking after his son Herbert (Stan Little) and his lodger Jacqueline Chantry (Nicolette Roeg), an orphan evacuee from the Channel Isles. The owner of a piano factory, Colonel Wright (H. F. Maltby) employs Jacqueline as a chauffeur, a job that would have been unknown for a female before the war. Colonel Wright's son Eric (Tony Pendrell) falls in love with Jacqueline but his mother (Hilda Bayley), who believes her son is too good for someone of Jacqueline's standing, frowns upon their affair. In the following extract, Jacqueline explains why she feels she is not good enough for him while he tries to reassure her with his hopes for the future.

Jacqueline: *"I'm wise enough to know that our friendship will find no favour in your parents' eyes".*

Eric:	*"Listen Jackie darling, we're living in a new world now, the war has cleared up a lot of things - I hope. "I was a Flight Lieutenant in the RAF but it didn't make any difference to the NCOs and men, we were all one. "And you were a motor driver in the ATS, you were all one weren't you".*
Jacqueline:	*"Yes we were".*
Eric:	*"Well that's how it must be now that all this is over. Class distinction didn't count in war and it mustn't count now".*

Mrs Wright in confronting Jacqueline tells of her displeasure at their closeness and firmly puts her in her place. With this, Jacqueline runs away and finds sanctuary at Pagoli's Nightclub. While simultaneously, Eric has travelled to the Channel Isles in a bid to trace Jacqueline's parentage. Upon his return with the news that Jacqueline is of French noble birth and is an heiress to a fortune, Eric's mother is overjoyed and presents Randle with the task of bringing her back. On their successful return, Eric and Jacqueline are reunited and she is welcomed into the family. The film shows that Eric held the same views of many of the younger generation in their hopes for a future classless society. His mother however, as with many of the older generation showed that it would still be sometime before it would be widely accepted. Following the film's narrative, it seems that Frank Randle played little part in it. Nevertheless, Randle weaves his way through the plot with many of his usual comic, ribald and smutty antics. He is seen getting drunk with Colonel Wright and shows his violent streak with his son Herbert, *"I've 'ad enough o' thee, if I get hold of you I'll spiflicate you. I'll tear your arms off and batter you over your ears with 'em. I'll pull your 'ed off and stuff it in your mouth".* On several occasions, Randle also offers to 'warm' the occasional female. Much is also made of the mix-up between the birth of quads to his wife and four puppies that a neighbour has asked him to drown. A trio of sidekicks aids Randle in several slapstick routines, these being music hall regulars Donovan & Byl and the male half of Arnley & Gloria. Two musical interludes are presented, one being at the exclusive Pagoli's Nightclub, to where Jacqueline had run away. Here, she is seen performing a very pleasant song and dance. Randle also manages to show some of his nifty footwork with his eccentric dancing. This is of course only after gaining entry to the club by representing himself as Prince Tampoori of Amphibia, complete with full military regalia. Donovan, Byl and

Arnley are also on hand as his bodyguards. Earlier in the film, the local Home Guard Reunion had provided the backdrop for the usual concert. This opens with a truncated version of Arnley and Gloria's dance act. The main entertainment however, is provided by the duo-pianists Rawicz and Landauer and a Song Scena in which soloist Helen Hill sang *'Home, Sweet Home'*.

Trade shown in August of 1945 *'Home, Sweet Home'* eventually hit the nation's screens shortly after the world conflict had totally ended with the Japanese surrender. Again, Butcher's Film Services carried out its national release, apart of course from Blakeley's home territory. Some time later Butcher's were also to release a 'short' film entitled *'Randle and all That'*. This film had a running time of approximately fifteen minutes and its subject matter had been originally shot for inclusion in the concert section of *'Home, Sweet Home'* but never used in that production. Its omission from the original film was probably simply one of running time, as the film on its initial release ran for a protracted 90 minutes. Indeed, when Butcher's re-released the film during 1948 further cuts were made. The contents of *'Randle and all That'* consisted of a fuller version of Arnley and Gloria's *'I've Got Rhythm'* routine, and Donovan & Byl performing their comic *'Tumbling Tomfoolery'* acrobatic act. Frank Randle as the star featured in a sketch entitled *'Randle Remembers'*. In this he depicts elderly Joe Higgins a boot and shoe repairer, a character based on 'Grandad' from his 'Grandpa's Birthday' sketch. This octogenarian was a much gentler character than his other 'old men' were. The scene opens as Joe enters his shop to the strains of 'Home, Sweet Home' indicating the film's pedigree. Here he reminisces first with his budgie and then with a series of customers. Together with one young woman, they discuss a subject that in the hands of the 'Old Hiker' would have been put over as lewd. Yet with Joe, Randle handles it moderately and talks with kindness, and with the punch line the young woman and the audience knows old Joe is only being humorous.

Young Woman:	*"Do you know old farmer Wilkinson's place? Well it's all fenced off and a sign up".*
Randle:	*"Aye! It's a nudist place they've got".*
Young Woman:	*"A nudist camp, in the village?"*
Randle:	*"Aye!"*
Young Woman:	*"It's disgraceful."*

Randle:	*"It is."*
Young Woman:	*"It is disgusting."*
Randle:	*"Aye!"*
Young Woman:	*"It ought to be shifted."*
Randle:	*"Aye, nearer my place."*
Young Woman:	*"Have you seen any of them?"*
Randle:	*"Yes I have."*
Young Woman:	*"You have."*
Randle:	*"Aye!"*
Young Woman:	*"You mean you've looked over and you've seen them?"*
Randle:	*"Looked over and seen 'em! I've been chucked out twice".*

With five screen appearances behind him, Randle was now firmly established as a film comedian as well as a stage performer, and was being lapped up by audiences. Now, he had become equally as popular as George Formby, even if only in the north. While Formby's 'gormless' humour was acceptable nationwide, that of Randle was less appreciated the further south it travelled. Randle did finally accomplish nationwide popularity, though this was ironically only achieved through the pages of the children's comic 'Film Fun'. Depending on the year, the comic billed him as the star of either Butchers or Mancunian films. Randle's caricature appeared for several years from the late 1940s through to the 1950s. So while his films and stage shows, may not have been welcomed too much in the south he still brought a smile to many a young southern face. Of course, there were many people living in England's southern counties who did enjoy Randle's film antics. While some would have to seek them out and travel miles to watch them, others were more fortunate to find a Randle film at their local cinema. Ken Treherne, in 1945 was a thirteen-year-old schoolboy living in Bristol. Like most youngsters of his age, Ken enjoyed nothing better than his Saturday trip to the Regal Cinema to watch the comedy films. Ken recalled, *"I enjoyed George Formby and Sydney Howard among others, but the wizardry best recalled was that of Frank Randle and the other Blakeley stars. Not so much for the material used but for their image. This was unreal, every other comic from that period, Bob Hope, Danny Kaye, it was the script content, but with Blakeley's comedies it was the imagery".* Comedian Bob Monkhouse once wrote, *"Growing up in Beckenham and Worthing in the prim and proper south...I would cycle for miles to the flea pits of Penge or the Moorish palaces of Brighton to sit in secret glee at*

Banner heading and enlarged frame from 'Film Fun' featuring
'Frank Randle Famous star of Mancunian Films'

the antics of Randle, 'King Twist' himself and the grotesque band of wonderful northern eccentrics". The late Leslie Halliwell noted writer and originator of the famous 'Halliwells Film Guide' referred to Randle in his book 'Seats In All Parts'. Bolton born Halliwell told of a visit during his teens to wartime Surrey and of his surprise at seeing a Randle film playing at the County Cinema, Weybridge. When Randle embarked on his usual ribald screen antics, Halliwell recalled, *"I would have laughed at home, but it did not seem proper to sink so low in Weybridge".*

After the release of *'Home, Sweet Home'* in August 1945 Blakeley was getting his next project, *'Under New Management'*, off the ground. For quite some time he had been faced with the reality that the cost of renting studio space had been ever rising and of the fact that it wasn't always available at a time when he needed it. Indeed, it was more through luck than planning that he managed once more to move into

Riverside. Though at the time he would have been unaware, that *'Under New Management'* would be his last film from a London studio. Whenever it was possible for him, Blakeley would work with people whom he knew and with whom he felt comfortable. Therefore, it was no coincidence to find that hosts of familiar names were involved with this production. He and Arthur Mertz were again responsible for the storyline. Geoffrey Faithfull was again enrolled, as cameraman while his chosen cast was almost identical to that of *'Demobbed'*, made just a year before. Incidentally, after making *'Demobbed'* two of its stars, who were also involved with *'Under New Management'*, went on to appear in a record-breaking panto season. Norman Evans and Betty Jumel opened in 'Humpty Dumpty', in December 1944 and their appearance at the Theatre Royal, Leeds was to be an unprecedented one. Their panto run was to last more than five months far exceeding any other panto season, even those of today. As the final curtain came down on 'Humpty Dumpty' Evans was ready for a summer season and also to join up again with Jumel, Nat Jackley, and Dan Young for the filming of *'Under New Management'*. In the film, Blakeley had cast Evans in the role of a chimney sweep who becomes a beneficiary of an old run down hotel. Evans with the help of his

**NAT JACKLEY · NORMAN EVANS
DAN YOUNG · BETTY JUMEL
— NICOLETTE ROEG —**

"HONEYMOON
HOTEL"

in

GUEST ARTISTE
CAVAN O'CONNOR
The Strolling Vagabond

*'Under New Management
was reissued in 1948 as
'Honeymoon Hotel'*

madcap former army buddies, Jackley and Young, soon start to bring the hotel to life. They are unaware however, that the hotel site has been designated for a development scheme that includes an airport, thereby vastly increasing the value of the property. Two villains armed with this information try to persuade Evans to sell, telling him the hotel and grounds are hardly worth anything. In an effort to help, a young accountant who happens to be in love with Evans' daughter, steps forward. All looks lost though, when the conmen and Evans discover that under the terms of his inheritance, Evans must pay a large sum or

*Norman Evans (Above) as Joe and Dan Young (Below) as Dan
in 'Under New Management - 1945*

surrender the lease. Support is at hand though when the necessary funds are found thanks to the young accountant's father. All of which brings a celebratory party, in the hotel's cocktail bar, where everyone joins in the toast to Evans' daughter and the accountant. The title of the film also to many had an underlying meaning as a new government was now running the country. *'Under New Management'* had its trade show in February of 1946 going on release shortly after. Even before *'Under New Management'* had started doing the rounds of the nation's cinemas, the Blakeley production machine was in action. On this occasion, though things were moving somewhat slowly. We have already stated that he had been unhappy about the rising costs of hiring London studios and he had become increasingly frustrated at having to pay even more should any of his productions over run, which they invariably did. Now after the war, the cost, to Blakeley's mind had soared, but the final decision to pay or not, never really materialised, as he simply could not find a studio in which to take his next production. Blakeley's future and consequently that of his two sons, Tom and John, was to be mapped out on a train journey. In the company of his eldest son Tom, the conversation centred on John Blakeley's total frustration at his present predicament. Here he was, a film producer unable to get into a studio to make his films. Of course, even if he had overcome that obstacle, it would have meant paying out even more money to do so. At some point during their journey, it was suggested that a move to Manchester could end this particular problem. If premises could be found to open studios of his own, Blakeley would also be able to provide work and security for his sons both recently out of service with the RAF. The idea of a Manchester studio was something Blakeley had once toyed with back in 1933. Even to the extent of trying to search out premises and backers. By the time the train had arrived at its terminus they had made a serious decision to try at least to get their idea off the ground. Looking back today, Tom's son Mike Blakeley recalls, *"that particular train journey resulted in the birth of the Manchester Film Studio and remained as one of my father's lifelong favourite memories"*. After giving more thought to the notion of opening his own studio, Blakeley and his sons set about the task of finding suitable premises. He knew however, that such a venture would need more financial backing than he alone could offer. Consequently, Blakeley sought out investors from the Lancashire business community. One of the first people to show an interest in Blakeley's venture was Jimmy Brennan who had originally started in business as a scrap metal dealer in his hometown of Barrow. Brennan, over the years had developed a keen interest in theatre and had invested in many shows. At this time, he also owned fourteen cinemas and his live theatres included the Hippodrome, Hulme (Manchester) and the Grand Theatre, Blackpool. With interest, Brennan informed Blakeley that if his studio idea should show signs of developing further then he would be willing to make an investment.

The search to find appropriate premises in Manchester turned out to be just as hard as trying to get studio space in London. There was also the certainty that any adaptable building they believed suitable would undoubtedly need extensive work carried out on it. Difficulties would arise here due to the shortage of materials and the fact that many building restrictions, imposed during the war years, were still in force. Undaunted they continued in their quest and it was only by chance that Blakeley came across the premises, which were finally to bring his dream to reality. A little more than a mile or so from Manchester city centre lay the quiet suburb of Rusholme and it was while travelling along Dickenson Road, one of its main thoroughfares, that Blakeley spotted a disused grey stone church. This run down building was once a Wesleyan Church and Sunday school built in 1862 by Charles Beswick for £2,000. Though when the three divisions of Methodism united during the 1930s many of the churches were disposed of. The Dickenson Road property had remained empty for quite some time, latterly being used as a wartime ARP centre. Examining the exterior, Blakeley could see the potential the church offered, with its separate parish hall and church house. On the day arranged to view the interiors, Blakeley took along with him several members of his family; being very close, he valued their opinion. Included in the party was Bernard Kelly, who after marrying Win Blakeley was of course John's son-in-law. Apparently, Bernard or 'Bud' as he was known, was the joker in the family, and seeing the marble altar immediately rushed to it and with exaggerated gesticulations mimicked a Mass. Whether, his religious father-in-law saw the funny side of this is unknown. Happy that he had found appropriate premises Blakeley's new company 'Film Studios Manchester Ltd', with Brennan as a director was now in effect up and running. When everything between the Company and the Church authorities was finalised, Blakeley wasted no time in engaging architect Joseph Gomersall to work on the conversion. One of the first tasks was the removal of the stained glass windows. Certainly not needed in a film studio John E. still knew their beauty and their worth and had no desire to see the windows destroyed. Therefore, he offered them freely back to the Methodist authorities and was prepared to transport them at his own expense. To John's surprise his offer was refused, although, as he once recalled, *"They were worth well over £1000 the colours of which could not be duplicated today. "I can't understand anyone not wanting them"*. After this refusal John offered them to the Roman Catholic authorities, which were more than happy to receive them, promising to install them in the next church they built.

The total cost of buying the church property and in making all the alterations came to around £25,000 a figure, which was to increase threefold before the studio was to open. This final amount included all the necessary equipment required to make the studio functional, there was the latest Marconi-Vistaone sound system, the Vinton cameras and dollies along with all the lighting equipment supplied by HD Industries. Then of course there were the countless smaller, but nonetheless, essential items needed for the smooth operation of a studio. In addition to all this expenditure, there was also the actual production cost, which was estimated at between £70,000 and £85,000.

Two other people joining the 'Film Studios Manchester' as directors were, like Jimmy Brennan, also cinema owners. Between them Harry Moorhouse (HDM Circuit) and J. Frederick Emery (J. F. Emery Circuit) owned around seventy cinemas at this time. Together with the fourteen cinemas owned by Brennan, this gave the Studio a ready market. Although being involved with the HD Moorhouse Company since its inception, Harry Moorhouse had only recently, on the death of his brother Herbert Douglas, become its Managing Director. Originally, chartered accountants in Manchester the brothers around 1909 moved into the cinema business. Herbert was the showman while Harry took more of a backroom role. From their first acquisition, the Pavilion, Chorlton, in 1909 the circuit had grown over the years to reach around forty cinemas by 1946.

The architect responsible for the conversion of the old church, Joe Gomersall, was also a director of two cinemas, these being the Roxy, at Hollinwood (Oldham) and the Roxy, at Hurst (Ashton-under-Lyne). He had also designed many other cinemas and was director of the Verona, at Guide Bridge (Ashton-under-Lyne), which only days before its scheduled opening he had sold to the Odeon Circuit. Gomersall's passion for cinema was evident to most people who knew him and

61

when he expressed a desire to work on the studio sets Blakeley readily appointed him as Art Director. He was also to join the board of directors.

The sixth and final member of the studio's board of directors was to be Frank Randle. It was Randle himself who made the suggestion to Blakeley, possibly because of the difficulties Randle was experiencing with the making of his current film 'When You Come Home', in production at Nettlefold Studios. The film was going way over budget (in the end it was to cost almost six-times as much as a Blakeley production) and perhaps more to the point from Randle's line of reasoning, was the fact that he thought the script was just not funny. The relationship between Randle and producer/director John Baxter was at breaking point and Baxter vowed never to work with him again. Of course, Randle had been far from perfect when making films for Blakeley, but no matter what the pair actually thought of each other, they at least had a working relationship. Blakeley therefore accepted Randle on to the board. For not only would the move bring further investment, Blakeley also knew that Randle was still a box office draw. By becoming a company director, Randle was virtually committing himself solely to Blakeley's productions, something that suited them both.

After the conversion of the old church was completed, the place was unrecognisable. The main body of the building, the church itself, was turned into the main stage measuring 100ft x 80ft, a balcony which overlooked this was soundproofed and fitted with the recording equipment and from this vantage point Kenneth Ross, the recording director, and W. Howell the recordist had a clear unobstructed view of the set below. The St. Helens firm 'FibreGlass Ltd' carried out soundproofing throughout the studio. This consisted of hard mattresses on the walls and ceiling being packed together with glass fibre wool all held in place by chicken wire. Although, this served its purpose as soundproofing it was also to provide future acoustical problems for the sound recordists. The smaller Parish Hall became the home for stage number two and was around 60ft x 40ft. All of the smaller rooms within the hall were also utilised becoming dressing rooms etc. Mary Waller, who was employed at the Parsonage when the studio conversion was taking place, informed us. *"I never thought it would materialise. I couldn't visualise what the end result would be. I mean it was basically a shell. I just could not visualise a film studio appearing there, but*

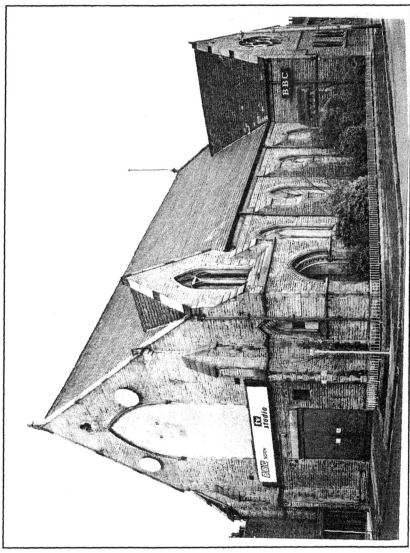

The old Wesleyan Church on Dickenson Road, home first to Film Studios Manchester and latterly the BBC.

when it did it was like a dream. It was very smart we had a gorgeous entrance with a commissionaire, there were two wonderful stages soundproofed from floor to ceiling; it was a thing I never thought I'd see in Manchester. We asked Ronnie Maasz who was to later work at the studio on several Frank Randle comedies, how the studio compared to the smaller London studios. *"In a way.* He replied. *"It would be a little unfair to compare the studios in Manchester with say Riverside or Walton. True there was not a great deal of difference in size but they were purpose built and had to cater for all types of film making with a sophisticated sound dock and props room etc, Manchester was purely used for the Blakeley type of film making".* Blakeley, speaking about the conversion told a newspaper of the period:*" I moved in with untried staff. Apart from photography and sound crew, I was about the only one with any experience of the film industry. "It was hard work, but eventually we managed to turn the church into a studio".*

The months of hard work by many people came to fruition on Monday 12th May 1947 when Blakeley achieved his ambition, as Manchester's first film studio was ready to open. While this was certainly an occasion for the city and for Blakeley, and although there was an impressive turnout for the opening ceremony, it surprisingly didn't receive such great news coverage. The local residents were out in force for they had never before seen anything like this. A touch of Hollywood was now right here on their own doorstep. To them, this was no ordinary Monday morning as a steady stream of expensive and impressive looking cars drove along Rusholme's streets on their way to the studio. A good-sized crowd stood and cheered as Frank Randle stepped from a sky blue Mercedes. George Formby delighted onlookers by stopping to sign autographs. Sandy Powell waved to the crowds, as no doubt he did over the next few weeks while filming at the studio. Sandy's co-stars on the studio's first production *'Cup-Tie Honeymoon'* were also present. Many of who were working on the film shortly after the opening speeches had been made. Once everyone had entered the building Robert Wilkinson Fox chairman of the Manchester branch of the Cinematograph Exhibitors Association gave an opening speech. The ceremony, which lasted less than two hours, also saw George Formby reminiscing on how Blakeley had put him into his first film as well as speeches from Sandy Powell and Frank Randle. While everyone was in high spirits for the occasion there was a little sadness in Blakeley's heart due to the death of Arthur Mertz who had passed away before the studio's opening day. Mertz however, had still played a part in the making of *'Cup-Tie Honeymoon',* having partly written the

64

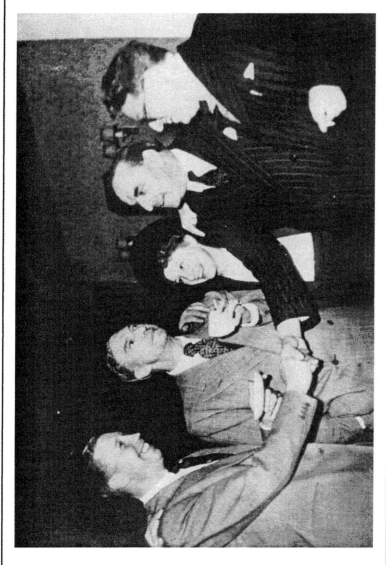

Pictured at the official opening of Film Studios Manchester are George Formby, Frank Randle, Joyanne Bracewell, John E. Blakeley and Sandy Powell.

65

story before his death. On the opening credits of the film, the screenplay was credited to Parson's and Toner. After Mertz's death, Harry Jackson took a hand in the scripting of *'Cup-Tie Honeymoon'* and was partly if not fully responsible for many future Blakeley films. Arthur Mertz had had a lifetime in showbusiness, first as a performer then as a writer, a producer and latterly as a journalist writing a weekly column for the theatrical paper 'The Performer'. These articles took the form of a journal or diary about the various artistes he had met that particular week. Therefore, anyone appearing at say, The Ardwick Empire, Manchester's Palace or Opera House, Theatre Royal, Stockport or any of the many northern theatres could find themselves written about. During the last months of his life, his son accompanied Arthur on many of these theatre visits. Arthur Mertz (junior) remembers: *"We often went to the Theatre Royal, Stockport. "There, in the very top bar, which we called the Crows Nest, there was a particular seat that my father always sat in. "From this chair, with a large John Haig whisky in his hand, he would dispense wisdom, advice and generally philosophise with all the up and coming artistes who were appearing at the theatre, all of whom would be sitting on the floor at his feet listening to his guidance".* The Reville brothers who owned the theatre had encouraged this and after Mertz (senior's) death, they had his chair polished and a plaque placed upon it bearing his name and the words 'seat of philosophy'. This chair now stands in the living room of Arthur Mertz (junior) and we had the privilege of sitting in it while we listened to several tales told by the younger Mertz. There is one wonderful story about Arthur Mertz senior, which was often told in showbusiness circles and was one which singer Donald Peers also recounted in his autobiography 'Pathway'. Arthur Mertz was a very large man weighing about 20 stone, however, he possessed a great dignity as big men very often do, and he had a lightness of foot and maintained a great courtesy. The story goes, big man as he was, he would glide into the theatre bar raise his homburg hat to the barmaid and say 'good evening my dear. 'May I have a large John Haig in a clean glass, a good measure, and is there anything to pay?' One particular night a quick-witted barmaid replied, 'Yes sir! But only for the use of the glass.' It was through his father that Arthur Mertz (junior) came to work for Blakeley in 1946 shortly after being demobbed from the army. Over the oncoming years, he was to have a variety of jobs at the studio but initially his job was to analyse the script and separate it, so the sets could be arranged ready for Joe Gomersall to start building them.

By 1946 Sandy Powell was a household name having already spent more than thirty years in the business. He had started even before he was in his teens appearing on stage as a boy-soprano and comedian. With his increasing appearances in the music halls and in panto seasons, he had become by the late 1920s very popular, achieving star status before the end of the decade. During the 1930s, he made many comic 78 rpm records, containing many of his music hall sketches, including 'The Lost Policeman' and 'Sandy Joins the Nudists'. He also made several recordings with Gracie Fields including 'Gracie's and Sandy's Party'. Radio heightened his popularity when the BBC put him on the air during 1928. From this developed regular monthly hour-long shows with varying titles. His famous catch phrase 'Can you hear me, Mother?' was born out of one of these shows, 'Sandy at the North Pole', and was to stick with him for the rest of his career. 'Can you hear me, Mother?' was also the title for his second feature film released in 1936. He made a further five film outings before being approached by John E. for his appearance in 'Cup-Tie Honeymoon'. The film also starred the inevitable Dan Young with Betty Jumel - making her third picture for Blakeley - and Pat McGrath.

Sandy Powell

The main plot involved an amateur international footballer (McGrath) who gives up the captaincy of England to turn out for professional club Rovers, in a cup-tie with local rivals United, when the regular centre forward is unable to play. His father, Harry Chambers, among other ventures owns several eating-houses and supper bars. McGrath proves to be the match winner scoring the winning goal from the penalty spot. Consequently, his delighted father gives his permission for him to marry his girlfriend whom he employs at one of his supper bars - hence the film's title. That is the basic story with the laughter aspect being provided by Powell, Young and Jumel in a sort of sub plot. Jumel is the owner of a boarding house where Powell and Young are staying. It is mainly here that the threesome's comic capers are carried out. There are good scenes set in a sub-post office and one in a supper bar with other cast members. Powell especially revels in these comical antics. Albert Stanbury wrote three original songs for *'Cup-Tie Honeymoon'* and Fred Harris provided the musical accompaniment and the incidental music. Wynne Mertz recalled, *"Apparently when the studio was opening Blakeley knew he needed musicians, so he got hold of Fred Harris, who was, at the time the Musical Director at the Palace Theatre, Manchester. Fred then found the instrumentalists to form an orchestra which essentially then became the studio orchestra".* Fred Harris was at this period quite well known in the business and was certainly a talented musician. Born in Brynamman, Wales, he had started out by playing for the films shown in his local cinema. He had made many BBC radio broadcasts and had become a popular performer on Manchester's dance scene, having played for various orchestras at such venues at the Winter Gardens.

Many of Blakeley's previous films had been processed at the Kay Film Laboratories in London. Here he had become well acquainted with the manager, Ernie Stimson. Meeting him one day, they were discussing the fact that Blakeley would soon be opening his own studio and that he was looking for a film editor. As it happened, this was the line of work in which his wife Dorothy was involved. Although she herself didn't know Blakeley, an arrangement for them to meet was organised and the outcome of this was an offer for her to come to Manchester for around ten weeks work on *'Cup-Tie Honeymoon'*. Dot Stimson recalling that time said: *" I had never been to Manchester before and I wasn't sure what to do. "However, I said yes and my ten weeks turned into seven years. "Blakeley said to me 'you'll love Manchester, you know there is some beautiful countryside nearby. "Which was really funny as all I ever saw were my digs and the studio. "I remember the day I arrived, there was no one there, they were all at a football match.* The game they had all been attending was one at Maine Road, Manchester, where the match between Manchester City and Aston Villa was being shot for inclusion in Cup-tie Honeymoon. According to Arthur Mertz they filmed the penalty shot separately with plenty of film extras involved, some in City shirts and some in what was supposed to be Villa's, but were in fact shirts borrowed from Burnley being the same colour. The filming of the penalty didn't quite work out as Blakeley had planned, for each extra that they tried as the goalkeeper were to slow in carrying out their action. Mertz remembers well Blakeley's reaction to this: "Where did you get this lot from he shouted? *"I informed him that they were all from an agency, well John E. answered back; well that bloody goalkeeper is just useless.* It was at this point that Arthur Mertz was to make the first of his own two appearances in the film. Putting on the goalkeeper's shirt he stood between the posts as Pat McGrath ran up to shoot a good shot which Arthur palmed down and away from goal. McGrath had to try again; this time Mertz tipped it over the bar much to Blakeley's annoyance. Mertz recalled: *"John E. cried, Arthur! You've got to miss it! He's got to score! "So I said to pat, put in down there and I'll make an effort and miss it."* Although filming on *'Cup-Tie Honeymoon'* was underway John E. continued visiting theatres. This was necessary as several minor roles in the production had still to be cast. It was from the various rep companies that he discovered the talented performers to fill these and the small parts of future pictures. In fact, the search for talent was never ending for Blakeley. He was continually looking for the stars that he could sign up for his films. Consequently, Arthur Mertz and Tom Blakeley under instructions from John E. one night visited the Garrick theatre, Southport. It was their brief to watch an artiste with a view to getting him under contract. After the show was over the two of them went back stage to talk with their target, Irish tenor Josef Locke. Within minutes, he had agreed to do a couple of films for Blakeley, the first being *'Holidays with Pay'.* Another night Blakeley asked Mertz to go along to Chorlton rep to run the rule over a female artiste. Mertz duly obliged, reporting that he thought the girl was good. That was enough for Blakeley to sign Pat Pilkington, who later as Pat Phoenix found fame as Elsie Tanner in the television soap opera Coronation Street. *"I was instrumental in giving her her first film part - 'two lines, a cough and a spit'",* as he described it. Blakeley also recruited another Rep actor, Bernard 'Bunny' Graham, a member of Frank Fortesque's Players. Together he and Pat made their first appearances in *'Cup-Tie Honeymoon'.* The surname of Graham was in fact simply a stage name used by Bernard Arthur Popley with 'Bunny' being the pet name given to him by his wife. He was later to change his name by deed poll to Bernard Youens and find fame as Stan Ogden in 'Coronation Street'. In the film, Bunny had the role of a chimney sweep with just around six lines of dialogue. He was also used as an extra in a cafe scene in which Pat, as Sandy Powell's wife also appeared. The extras for Blakeley's films were either obtained from an

John E. in trademark Homburg and son Tom Blakeley (centre) surrounded by studio and film crew at the conclusion of filming on 'Cup-Tie Honeymoon'. Behind Tom is film editor Dot Stimson with Arthur Mertz at her side (right). Wynne Donlan is seated left of John E. While front row (left of clapperboard) is Bert Tracey.

agency or were just friends or family members of the people who worked for him. They literally could have been picked up off the street. Wynne Donlan, who was later to marry Arthur Mertz (junior), recollects: *"Bert Tracey lived back to back with me in Victoria Park, Manchester. "He came out into the garden one morning and called out to me. "He said 'would you like to appear at the film studios, we've got a cafe scene and we need some young ladies to sit in the cafe'".* Bunny Graham and Pat Pilkington were both featured in this same scene. They assigned all the young ladies boyfriends to sit with and Wynne was given Bunny. *"He was a very handsome boy, almost a replica of Clarke Gable"*, Wynne recalled. Unfortunately, appearing as an extra brought problems for Wynne. She was in employment and had only agreed to do the filming because it was just to be for one day. *"At the end of the day when they'd finished the filming we all had food on our plates"*, said Wynne. *"Which was marvellous when it was first brought in. "But during the shooting, you'd only get it so far towards your mouth before they'd shout cut. "You then had to wait for them to shout action again. "This was going on all day and if the scene was not completed, they said everyone who had been in it had to report back next morning. "I explained that I couldn't come back as I'd already played wag from work for that day".* Arthur Mertz explained to Wynne, and the others, that as they were now in the scene they would all have to come back otherwise the continuity would be wrong. Wynne said: *"When I told my mother she was furious that I needed a second day off work. "She said 'do what you want but if you lose your job that's your problem'. "Well I went back the second day and we did the scene again, by this time however, the food was beginning to smell, but they couldn't move it because it would throw the continuity out. "We suffered the smell of the food all day which was pretty bad as the arc lights made the place extremely warm". "Then at the end of the day...well blow me, because Sandy Powell and Betty Jumel couldn't get their lines right they shouted, 'everyone in this scene...back here tomorrow'. "That was really bad for me as a third day off work needed a sick note and I knew I couldn't get one as I wasn't really ill".* When Wynne told Arthur Mertz of her problem, he suggested she should see Tom Blakeley to explain things to him, and the outcome of her doing so effectively changed her life. For not only did she end up working at the studio, she was eventually to get to know and later marry Arthur Mertz. She said: *"I remember telling Tom of my predicament and he asked me what kind of work I did. "I told him I was a bookkeeper, cashier. "He asked if I did wages, so I said yes. "He then asked could I do them for him, when I said I could he told me to come back to finish the filming and then to report on the following Monday to start work for him." "I stayed at the studio until it closed".* Another method used by

71

Blakeley to recruit people for his pictures was to hold auditions, usually though these were only held when children needed to be found. With the making of *'Cup-Tie Honeymoon'* well in progress, Blakeley decided to hold a series of auditions in the hope of discovering a young talent. Arthur Mertz said of these: *"Mothers brought their daughters along and among them was a pretty little girl who did a number and I was impressed. "I told Blakeley and we gave her a test. "He liked her so he gave her a little part in the film, in fact as it turned out it was a fairly decent part actually and her name was Joyanne Bracewell"*. Bert Tracey was quoted at the time as saying: *"Joyanne has an amazing personality we think in a few years she will be our regular leading lady"*. This though, was not the way things were to turn out. Joyanne, for whatever reason never pursued a career in acting. Instead, she carried on with her academic studies and eventually qualified as a barrister. Today, as a Judge and Dame of the British Empire, the Honourable Joyanne Bracewell DBE recalled: *"I did appear in films, the names of which I have long forgotten. "I was about twelve years old. "I am afraid they were very third rate productions"*. Looking back Joyanne was a local girl with a difference and what a difference that was. From her early childhood, her destiny was almost mapped out for her, as she was guided to reach the pinnacle of success in one form or another. She never attended school being taught instead privately at home by tutors. To say she was a bright young person would be an understatement. Even in the leisure activities she pursued, and for one of such a young age, she became an expert in all she did, be it acting, riding, dancing or swimming. She told us that the films for Blakeley followed on from some BBC Children's Hour work she had done. Joyanne had played alongside a mainstay of the Northern Children's Hour, Wilfred Pickles in *'The Young Stranger'*, which was broadcast in 1944. This play, which Nan McDonald produced in the North, was often repeated by popular request. Radio listeners also heard Joyanne in Muriel Levy's serial adaptation of E. Nesbitt's, *'Five Children and It'* the first post-war serial to be heard from the north. Joyanne's performance in *'Cup-Tie Honeymoon'* had several critics giving her a far better review than the film itself. She continued to win people over with another highly commendable performance in *'Holidays with Pay'*. At this stage of her short film career, almost everyone believed that she was indeed a star in the making. Though after *'Holidays with Pay'* had been completed and had its trade showing Joyanne Bracewell the 'promising starlet' slipped quietly away from the show business scene.

Once established in Manchester, Blakeley was to take full advantage of the local surroundings for exterior shots. On one occasion for *'Cup-Tie Honeymoon'*, he was using Abney Hall in Cheadle, Cheshire, which then belonged to the Watt family of S & J Watt's Textiles. Abney Hall was later to become the Town Hall, of Cheadle. The camera had been set up to shoot the chairman of the football club leaving the house with his wife and getting into his car to go to the football match. Unfortunately, they also caught on film the Watt's butler who opened the door for the two actors. Arthur Mertz pointed this out to John E. informing him that as they'd caught him on camera they would need the butler for the reverse shot (the house interior) to be filmed in the studio. John E. disagreed with this until he viewed the rushes the next day, when he declared Mertz to be correct and that they did indeed need the butler. Obtaining the services of the real butler would have been impossible, so a substitute was urgently required. Blakeley informed the dozen or so technicians that were sitting in the little viewing theatre that what they needed was a fellow about five foot six inches tall and going bald. All eyes immediately looked towards Arthur Mertz. Consequently, he made a second appearance in the film as the butler in the interior shot.

Josef Locke the Irish tenor (centre) was, signed by John E. Blakeley (right) to appear in several films. John Blakeley junior is also pictured (left) with Tom Blakeley (front).

Chapter Four

It was on 29th September that Frank Randle, Tessie O'Shea and Josef Locke made their first appearances at the studio for the shooting of *'Holidays with Pay'*. Locke, who had previously done a few shows in his native Ireland, had been persuaded to try his luck over in England. It had been in 1945 at the Victoria Theatre, London that he made his English debut. Working for Jack Hylton in The Crazy Gang show, he displayed a talent, which soon was to gain him a worldwide audience. Josef Locke whose real name was Joseph McLaughlin was considered an ideal artiste for variety theatres on the Northern-England circuit. He had signed to Blakeley at a Southport Theatre, but Blackpool was where he was to really make his mark. The first of numerous summer seasons was made in 1946 as support to George Formby. Locke liked the town so much he eventually bought a house there, moving his family over from Ireland. The topical title of the film, *'Holidays with Pay'* was recognising the fact that at this period the British workforces were for the first time, enjoying their own holidays with pay. The holiday in this instance is the one taken by the Rogers family who like many northern families were heading off to Blackpool. Jack and Pansy Rogers, as played by Frank Randle and Tessie O'Shea, along with their daughter Pam (Sally Barnes) and brother-in-law Phil (Dan Young) all make the journey in a dilapidated old car. It is during the journey that Pam meets up with Michael Sandford (Sonny Burke) thereby introducing the love interest element to the film. Michael it is revealed is to inherit the family estate, but to do so he first has to spend a night in a mansion, which is reputed to be haunted. After arriving in Blackpool, and after several of Randle's antics, it isn't long before their boarding house landlady asks the family to leave. Because of this, the family joins Michael in his stay at the haunted house. Here they encounter an assortment of 'things that go bump in the night' including a ghost, a skeleton and an Egyptian mummy - all good fun as far as the audiences were concerned. Having spent the night at the house Michael finally inherits the estate and wins' Pam's hand in marriage. Josef Locke's appearance in this film does not involve him in any acting; he simply appears as a singer in an end of pier show, which also features the Rogers' family. Sally Barnes and Sonny Burke together sing *'The Natural Thing to Do'*, before Locke is introduced in a rather peculiar Western scene. It is peculiar in the sense that although it is set in a Wild West saloon, apart from one song everything else about it is Irish. Locke is introduced as 'Singing Paddy Flynn', the

74

barman is named Murphy and Locke even orders a couple of 'Murphy's' [Whiskey], this is all just before bursting in to song with *I'll Take You Home Again Kathleen'*. Locke performs a second song *'Moonlight and a Prairie Sky'*, specially written by Albert Stanbury, which probably gives explanation as to why a Western setting was used. Tessie O'Shea sang two numbers *'Strolling by the Seaside'* and *'He Isn't Much to Look At'*. Unfortunately, the only surviving copy of this film today seems to be a Butchers re-issue print, which has both Tessie O'Shea's songs and Locke's *I'll Take You Home Again Kathleen'* missing.

Tessie O'Shea is a scene from 'Holiday's with Pay'

What must it have been like working at the studio? Blakeley himself had said he'd opened with inexperienced staff. So if we assume that he along with the technical staff were the only ones with any experience, how did everyone else manage? It must have been quite a hectic baptism, for in the nine months since the opening of the Dickenson Road premises three films had been completed. Blakeley as the studio magnate, producer/director was perhaps a little eccentric especially in his dress sense. Wynne Mertz said of Blakeley: *"He'd been brought up the rough way. "His son Tom was a different kettle of fish to his father. "He was always immaculately dressed, had been sent to a good school and had been well educated"*. Although he was an astute businessman, John E Blakeley's main concern, was what was happening on the set. While knowing what was going on it seems he left the mundane running of the daily business routines to others. Those people he'd employed to do the job. On her first day at the studio, no one instructed Wynne Mertz about what exactly she had to do. John E. quite often never informed the office staff about contracts, how long artistes were booked for, and of concern to Wynne how much they were to be paid. Consequently, she would turn to Tom, and he would always manage to sort out many of the problems. Fridays were paydays at the studio and one funny moment sprang to Wynne's mind as we spoke of *'Holidays with Pay': "I remember a particular Friday when, being pay day, I had to go down and pay all the electricians and joiners. "Well they had been filming the haunted house sequence and there were lots of coffins and mummy cases all propped against the wall. "Suddenly the boys had a brainwave and they pounced on me and they pushed me into a mummy case. "With the top slammed shut, they laid the case out flat on the floor. "Just then Arthur Mertz came along and asked them who's in the box. "They told him it was me and he said get her out quickly. "As they opened the lid, I was lying there just like a mummy. I had my arms folded across my chest with all their wage packets fanned out like a pack of cards in my hands"*. Stories like this one would suggest that it was a fun place to work. Indeed, it soon became known as the 'fun factory' or 'Jollywood' and acquired a reputation as having a family feeling within the place. Everyone who worked there felt part of this family with John E. Blakeley as the father figure. Although to most people, he was just John E. (pronounced Johnnie), Dot Stimson and several others called him 'Pops'; Randle occasionally called him 'Dada' while naturally to Tom and John Jnr. he was simply Dad. The family feeling is one that is still remembered by many today. Mary Waller recalled, *"The family feeling was something already evident at the Parsonage, even before the studio had opened, it was here that we carried out all the ground work, the scripts, financing, contracts etc. "I used to make a daily trek from the Parsonage to the studio to collect information and type Mr Blakeley's correspondence"*. This would have been a difficult task for Mary, as Blakeley never left the set when a film was in production. According to Wynne Mertz, John E.

never came up to her office, she told us: *"I recall saying to Tom things like 'your dad's not told me about this contract, how long are they here for. What have I got to pay them, or will it be pro-rata?' "Tom would always help and tell me what I needed to know. "Then there were times that I needed to get Blakeley's signature on cheques. They'd be filming on the set and I'd have to wait till the red light went off before I could go in. When the light eventually went off, I'd seize my opportunity and go in. Mind you, I could guarantee that when I was inside he'd shout 'right, camera' and the red light would go back on and I'd be trapped inside the studio. "Eventually after the light went out again I'd manage to ask 'can you sign this cheque now for me Mr Blakeley', and he'd say 'yes give it to me', and he'd lean on my back while he signed. In fact you could never get to grips with him properly because he was such a busy man and didn't want to be bothered with what was going on in the offices".* The 'family feeling', which the studio generated, was brought about by the friendliness and the close-knit working relationship between employees; Along of course, with the fact that many were indeed related, either through blood or marriage. Besides the obvious Blakeley family connection of John E. and his two sons Tom and John. There was also Blakeley's son-in-law Bernard (Bud) Kelly who worked as prop and studio manager. Arthur Mertz had been introduced to Blakeley through his father's long-term connection with himself and Blakeley. As stated, Arthur Mertz was also to marry Wynne Donlan after meeting at work. John Mertz, Arthur's brother was employed at the studio as a boom operator. Mary Waller had her own sister as an assistant, while their brother, John was employed at the studio as a joiner on the sets. That same 'family feeling' which pervaded the studio even spread out into the local community. Many locals appeared as extras, usually as part of a crowd for which they received a guinea (£1.05p) a day. If they had one or two speaking lines, they would receive three guineas a day. Local residents also often came to the rescue regarding props; if they needed something urgently, Blakeley would often ask those living close to the studio to help. The residents absolutely loved it, especially the people from the local off-license, whose daughter ran the studio canteen; their trade always increased when a film was in production. As too, did that of the Welcome Inn, a local pub that became known as 'stage two' to everyone who worked at the studio. Most of the employees and stars, especially after work, would meet at the Welcome. Everyone that is except the Blakeleys', for John E. and his sons didn't mix socially after work. On the studio set John E. was unlike other directors, with his coloured shirts with the ever present arm bands, waistcoat and braces; when actually directing he would wear his 'directing jacket' a leather

77

zip-up flying jacket. He hardly ever left his director's chair from where he shouted out his orders. Apparently, his voice could be very loud even when speaking normally. He was a very formidable man and a hard taskmaster who on occasion could be most awkward. Behind his black spectacles, which he often wore, were piercing eyes, though there was always a twinkle there. When people saw that twinkle they knew something was going to happen, for Blakeley could always see a joke and he would find jokes anywhere, even if people played jokes on him. As a producer he knew what the audiences wanted, he was after all a grass roots northerner himself in tune with northern humour, and he knew how to put it into his films. While the scripts he worked from contained funny dialogue there were many blank pages, on which the words 'BUS.', 'BUSINESS', or 'ANY OTHER BUSINESS' was typed. It was at this point that the comedians of the film were to insert some of their own funny routines. They would have around twenty minutes to work out what they would do, mostly though it was just ad-libbed coming off the cuff. Blakeley knew how much material he wanted on film and he'd urge them to keep it going until he shouted 'cut'. There would be times during filming that Blakeley would stray from the script -not into the scheduled 'Business' routines - but parts where he would simply say 'forget the script lets do this', then inserting another comic situation he would urge 'go on be funny'. It has been said that Blakeley only ever filmed in long shot. While fundamentally true, this was not always the case. Dot Stimson pointed out that they had three cameras, one would be taking the master or long shot with the others being for medium and close-up shots. The various 'Business' routines were always done in long shot. This was mainly done because the stars were ad-libbing and Blakeley unaware of what was going to happen did not want to miss any of the action. Frank Randle having already made four films for Blakeley and now a director of the studio would more than anyone have known how the man worked. Undeniably, their relationship was really a love/hate one, going back to their days together in the London studios. Mary Waller suggested that Randle did not like to be directed: *"He liked to do things his own way on set,"* she said. *"Whenever Blakeley stopped him for something or other Frank would just leave the set halting the production until he returned"*. It was a part of Arthur Mertz's duties to get artistes onto the set whenever they required them, most of these were no trouble, but Randle was different. In a situation similar to the one described by Mary Waller, it would have been up to Arthur to try to coax Randle back to work. *"Now of course I had to be careful how I treated him"* Said Arthur: *".... after all he was a director of the*

78

company. *"Anyway, I'd go into his dressing room to try to talk him into going back on set. He'd say 'have a drink', so I'd join him in a bottle of Guinness. "We'd have an easy and amiable chat and eventually I'd ask if he was coming back onto the set. He'd say 'all right then Arthur' and he'd come down onto the set. "However, the instant he arrived back John E. would shout 'right break for lunch'. "That was Blakeley sort of getting his own back really and that was the sort of thing that happened between them day after day".* Blakeley and Randle could argue about almost anything and as Arthur added: *"This usually resulted in Randle storming off to his dressing room".* Wynne recalls that Randle even had a punch ball in his dressing room: *"Every time he was annoyed with Blakeley he'd knock hell out of this ball, you could hear him saying 'you bloody Blakeley you.... you bloody so and so'. "I caught him on a few occasions. I could hear him talking and punching away but when I'd knocked at the door and entered there'd be no one else there just him. He'd look at me and say 'Oh. I'm just having a go at Blakeley. He's got me all worked up again'. "You see the atmosphere between them could sometimes be quite explosive".* Frank Randle lived in Blackpool with his wife Queenie, but while filming *'Holidays with Pay',* he stayed in a caravan with his 'lady friend' actress Sally Barnes, who was also in the picture. Each Friday Jimmy Monroe, Frank's chauffeur, would go to a local florist to collect two beautiful bouquets of flowers, which Frank had ordered. Jimmy would bring them back to Wynne's office where he had to write out the cards for Frank. One read, 'To my darling Queenie - With all my love'. The other read, 'To my darling Sally...Love you forever'. Jimmy said to Wynne one Friday, 'My God Wynne if ever I get these cards mixed up there'd be a riot'. He then had to go down and give one bouquet to Sally before driving himself home to Blackpool and dropping the other off for Queenie on the way.

The filming of *'Holidays with Pay'* had taken a total of ten weeks to shoot, being completed during the first week of December. By this time, Mancunian had arranged the Manchester trade showing for *'Cup-Tie Honeymoon'.* An invited audience of stars, critics and the usual cinema owners and managers all gathered on the morning of Friday 16th January 1948 at Jimmy Brennan's Deansgate Cinema. The cinema incidentally was situated only a few minutes walk from Blakeley's offices at the Parsonage.

Tom Blakeley being the eldest son had by now gained considerable experience of filmmaking and was making head roads into the

79

*Trade Show announcement for 'Cup-Tie Honeymoon' January 1948.
Note the claim of 12,000 bookings for the previous Blakeley productions.*

80

production side. On the studio's first productions, he had worked alongside his father, firstly as Production Manager then on 'Holidays with Pay' as Assistant Director. Eleven years his junior, his brother John was relatively new to the industry and from the studio opening was mainly learning as he went along. Aiming for a career as a cameraman, John began initially learning about the cameras themselves, the fundamentals of operation and maintenance. By the time the shooting of 'Holidays with Pay' was underway, he was working as the second camera operator, with Gerald Pullen on first camera. With time, he was to acquire enough expertise to become head of the camera department, with the added responsibility of keeping the temperamental Vinten Cameras in running order. During the filming of 'Holiday's with Pay', John E. arranged for his younger son to take a camera crew to film at Manchester's Belle Vue. Here under the watchful eye of Gerry Pullen, John could gain further practice of camera work while shooting scenes in the Zoo, Ballroom, Gardens, and various acts at the Circus. The undertaking not only gave young John more useful experience behind the camera, but also supplied some useful film footage. From this, Tom was to eventually compile two documentaries 'International Circus Review' and 'Showground of the North'. One school of thought intimates 'International Circus Review' was conceived to include a storyline. Indeed, it has been suggested that certain studio scenes were actually shot for inclusion. Nevertheless, we can find no evidence to substantiate this. Arthur Mertz in remembering these films said, *"I indeed recall during 'Holidays with Pay' John being sent with a second unit camera crew to Belle Vue to shoot some scenes for a documentary to be completed later. "I did actually see the 'rushes' of these shots before editing and cutting, and I remember one of the crew humorously referring to the shots as 'Animals with Pay!' But I have no recollection at all of any storyline being inserted"*. Neither too, did the film editor Dot Stimson when we put the same question to her. One trade paper in reviewing the film described it simply as a *'Straightforward photographed version of the circus at Belle Vue'*; there was certainly no mention of storylines or actors. Throughout its 45-minute running time, the film featured a variety of circus acts including performing horses, acrobats, clowns, and a chimp, which wandered happily around the audience. Lacking a commentary, the soundtrack consisted solely of a musical background. The aim of *'Showground of the North'* was to take the cinema audience on a conducted tour of Belle Vue, showing off all it had to offer; a task, which it managed to do quite adequately with its informative commentary, spoken by Lionel Marsden. The film shows the Zoo with its variety of animals, and a look around the Gardens. Sports fans were treated to shots of the Speedway and a Rugby match. There were the inevitable shots of the famous Belle Vue Fun Fair before the film reached its close with a grand display of Fireworks.

Since opening, the studio had been busy and that is how Blakeley hoped it would remain. He already had another starring vehicle for Randle lined up *'The Girl at the High School'* and there was even talk of the studio being leased out. It had been reported that discussions with Dublin Films were at an advanced stage and they looked set to produce *'My Wife's Birthday'* at Rusholme sometime in April. The second week of March saw the Mancunian Film Corporation with a unique situation. Both *'Cup Tie Honeymoon'* and *'Holidays with Pay'* were to receive concurrent trade screenings at various cities throughout England, Scotland and Wales. On Tuesday 9th March, they showed *'Holidays with Pay'* in both Manchester and Sheffield while simultaneously they were screening *'Cup Tie Honeymoon'* in Birmingham, Glasgow, Liverpool, Newcastle and Nottingham.

Before the move to Manchester, the professional critics had never reviewed Blakeley's films kindly. If anyone at this stage was under the impression this would now change, they were to be sadly mistaken. The first two offerings out the Rusholme studio were again greeted with much adverse criticism. Even the northern press and in particular those of Blakeley's home city scarcely had a good word for either production. *"...this is hardly the stuff to make Hollywood take notice"*, (Manchester Evening Chronicle). *"...a mere stringing together of comic situations to suit the backwoods of Oswaldtwistle and other remote places. This is not the stuff of which big films are made,"* (Manchester City News). Almost everyone seemed to be looking for, or rather, expecting, Blakeley's films to be something more than he himself ever meant them to be. Not under any circumstances was he aiming for Hollywood. He certainly never intended them for the 'La-di-da' clique in London, as he called them. He made his films for a specific audience and the films were finding their market. By the time *'Holiday's with Pay'* was being screened to the paying public, at least one journalist, Ross Shepherd, had sat up and taken notice at how popular the film and its star Frank Randle actually was with the northern audiences. So much so, that through his paper the 'Sunday People' he hit out at J. Arthur Rank. It was his opinion that the vast amount of money Rank was spending on film production was not what the millions of cinemagoers wanted. *'You've got it all wrong Mr. Rank'*, screamed the headline, - *'they want Randle not Shakespeare!'* Ross Shepherd had travelled the north of England to gather his information first-hand by joining with the cinema queues and speaking to the people. He was soon to acknowledge the fact that Randle's *'Holiday's with Pay'*, and Formby's *'Off the Dole'* (made ten years earlier and still being screened) had people flocking to the cinema, and attendances for these were far outnumbering the Rank epics, which had cost far more to produce. Shepherd wrote, *"We've all been so busy making and praising 'Hamlet' and 'Henry V' that we have not understood that the factory workers and their wives much prefer to go to the pictures to see Frank Randle".* He went on to say, *"Are then the critics and Mr Rank always wrong?"* *"Not at all* - he continued - *the filmgoers of Oldham and Huddersfield like the rest of us always enjoy the gay romances of Anna Neagle and Michael Wilding".* *"Just as they are admirers of all the top dozen favourites when they are in parts that mean something".* Another irate cinemagoer, from Huddersfield told him. *"You people on the newspapers like the queerest sort of pictures, you must be a lot of highbrows who think we go to the pictures as if we were visiting an art gallery. "I'm sure we don't care who the director is or whether he has thought up some new way of using a camera".* Shepherd was to admit that he had previously always thought on a different level to these cinemagoers. Now through his article he was pointing out, that Rank too should be aware that he was also wrong in his way of thinking. Thousands upon thousands of pounds was being spent by Rank in comparison to the meagre pittance spent on the likes of Randle's films; yet, they were continually coining it in at the box-office. The author concluded by saying, *"One of these days he* [Rank] *should slip quietly away from the Dorchester Hotel and have a chat with the queues outside his cinemas in Preston and Pudsey. I am quite sure he would come back and fire all his scriptwriters who live in Kensington Gore".*

As April approached and nothing more having come from the talks with Dublin Films, Blakeley was himself back in the studio. On 5th April, production commenced on *'That's My Man'* starring Frank Randle. The previously proposed production for Randle of *'The Girl at the High School'* was rescheduled for a later date. Ben Hart the cinematographer on *'Holidays with Pay'* was back for this new production. On this occasion however, Ernest Palmer joined him. Having many years of experience behind him, Ernie Palmer knew the business inside out and was regarded by many as wasting his talents on the likes of Blakeley's productions. Work was nevertheless at this time, becoming increasingly thin on the ground and Ernie was quite happy doing any sort of film, John Blakeley's were no exception. Indeed this was to be the first of several films that Ernie was to work on at Manchester. Why there should have been the need for two cinematographers is not known. Perhaps John E. was not totally happy with Ben Hart's previous effort, for in Wynne Mertz's opinion, *"Ben Hart was a really flashy man who wasn't particularly good at his job"*. Apparently, his lighting direction was poor and John E. one day had cause to summon the crew and camera operators into his office because as he saw it 'something about the film just wasn't right'. Wynne actually wrote a little parody about the situation, which she sang to the tune of 'Oh What a Beautiful Morning'... *'Oh what a beautiful morning/ Oh what a beautiful day/ I've got a terrible feeling something will go wrong today/ To the office the crew go in crushes/ 'Cos there's something gone wrong with the rushes/ The camera's alright which gives Ben a fright/ Because he knows his gauzio isn't quite right/ Maybe J.B. will forget it perhaps he just must have his say/ But maybe the fault of the lighting is the shadow from Tessie O'Shea'.* Everyone thought this was extremely funny and they all wanted a copy. Of course, the whole thing had to be kept a secret from poor Ben Hart, who seemingly was the one at fault. The problem was with the way he had lit the set. Working alongside both Palmer and Hart on *'That's My Man'* were the two camera operators, Robert Foley and Robert Moss. John Blakeley junior operated the second camera assisted by A. Roberts and J.G. Nowell. Terry Cotter was the sound mixer and as always Dot Stimson was the sound and picture editor. One day during shooting John E. could hear the sound of paper tearing. Looking around he caught sight of Terry Cotter who was ripping and screwing up pages of the script and throwing them to the floor. Terry was annoyed that John E. had again strayed from the script making his job more difficult. John E. looked down at the crumpled papers and pointing to one saying, 'well that one is in'. Terry of course immediately picked it up, and smoothing out the crumpled page looked at it, only to see a blank page except for the one magic word 'Business' typed across it. Harry Jackson and Arthur Mertz Junior wrote the script for *'That's My Man'*, with the official credits also naming Frank Randle, though some would suggest that this be debatable. Randle was obviously the star of the picture being supported by Tessie O'Shea, Josef Locke, Jimmy Clitheroe, Sally Barnes and Syd & Max Harrison.

Syd and Max Harrison at this time had become one of the country's top comedy double acts, but it was as tap dancers that they originally made their show business debut. To those who remember these two mad Irishmen their story is one worth telling and although not wanting to digress too much we make no apology to briefly relate this to you. Brothers' Syd and Max were born in the South of Ireland, later moving to Belfast. Syd became a Charleston champion and Max a champion clog dancer. While still in their teens they decided to try their hand at the English music hall and having no written music for their first booking literally just busked it. Their tap dancing talent had literally been learnt from watching the hot movies of the day, including the series of 'Gold Diggers' films. The brothers' stayed in the cinema watching the films repeatedly until they had the rhythms in their head and could then transfer the same to their feet. The comedy aspect of their act began by accident as one night in the middle of a challenge routine a row started between them. It began with a push and a shove, this precipitated further pokes, and then sparks began to fly. Still doing their dance, Syd had his jacket ripped off by Max and then their shirts got ripped. In true show business fashion, there happened to be a theatrical booker in the audience who thought their 'comedy routine' was the funniest he'd ever seen. With the offer of work for their 'comedy act', the pair had to try to remember just what it was that they had actually done. This then was their start in comedy, and before long, they were headlining and topping bills across the country. Max was a natural born comedian; he was a funny man, as opposed to just delivering the funny lines. It has been said that they never rehearsed their routines; they just had an idea of what they wanted to do and ran with it. This then was probably the reason why later they found it hard to transfer to television, as they never could stick to time. Throughout their lives the brothers' were so very close to each other, both finished up separated from their wives and eventually lived together in a flat in Brighton bought for them by their sons Mike and Albie – well known comedians in their own right as Hope and Keen. As Syd's son Mike Hope recalled, *"their furniture was gambled away twice - when my father took ill with lung cancer Uncle Max screamed at him to get up and do a routine just to annoy the neighbours in the flat below. Dad was too far-gone and it wasn't long after that he sadly died. "Uncle Max, at the funeral, said to me that he was finished too and just wanted to be with his brother. Six weeks later, he was himself in hospital, with the doctors saying he was dying of a broken heart, they couldn't think of any other reason. Two weeks later he died".* During the filming of 'That's My Man', Randle had invited Syd and Max to Blackpool to proudly show them his yacht, the

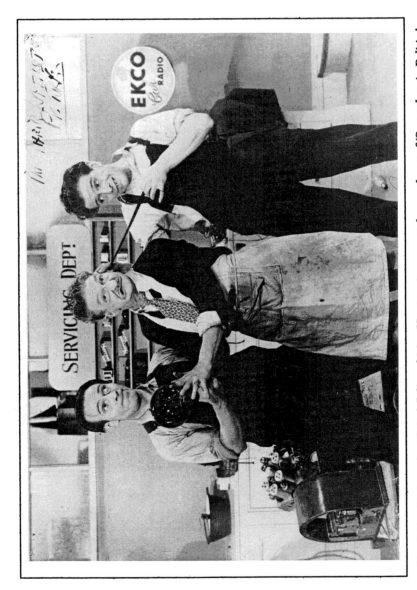

Frank Randle (centre) with Syd (left) and Max Harrison in a scene taken on the set of 'Somewhere in Politics'.

Nomura a converted lifeboat. Although he may have had a yearning to be a seafarer, Randle was in fact hopeless at the task. He had mainly obtained his vessel as a means of keeping up with the Formby's and to impress the Blackpool show business elite. Ordered to wear full naval uniforms Syd and Max Harrison joined Randle on deck as he attempted to sail up to the central pier at full tide. Unfortunately, Randle got it wrong and as the tide turned the boat's hull broke as it went to ground. Frank of course made light of this, for he had done what he had intended, he had shown everyone he was 'Jack the Lad', up there with the best of them.

In *That's My Man'* Randle plays Joe Smart who along with his wife Daisy (Tessie O'Shea) and their son Reggie (Sonny Burke) arrive at their new house to discover that it has also been let to someone else, Martha Parker (Bunty Meadows) and her brothers (Syd and Max Harrison). The representative from the estate agent, Marjory Willoughby, suggests that they should share the home. With the discovery that both Daisy and Martha belong to the 'Women's Freedom League' they agree to the idea. Marjory's father (Locke) is the owner of a local radio shop where Joe is employed, along with Howard the store manager. Joe manages to ruffle Mr Willoughby's feathers by standing against him in a local election. Howard manages to reassure Willoughby that Joe will not win, much to his delight. In order to keep his promise to his employer, Howard frames Joe for theft. But Reggie, who has fallen in love with Marjory, thwarts his evil doings. Mr Willoughby although actually losing out to Joe in the election unites their families by giving his consent to Reggie and Marjory's romance. In playing Mr Willoughby, Josef Locke earning a hefty £1,000 a week, was probably the highest paid star at the studio at that time. Frank Randle, although a director of the studio also received a weekly salary while filming, earning a little less than Locke at around £850 a week. The two stars having worked together and both living in Blackpool had become good friends. Indeed, jointly they had gained for themselves a reputation for their womanising, gambling, all-night drinking sessions and general rowdiness. While having his performers under contract, Blakeley would also utilise their talents by booking several of them into local theatres for a week or two. Josef Locke, who besides working at the studio, was also booked to appear at the Ardwick Hippodrome, giving him a very exhausting performing schedule. Having spent the daytime at the studio and the evening at the theatre, Joe one time decided to finish off the night with a drink.

Apart from the usual 'Welcome Inn' there was another pub called the 'Bay Horse' on Wilmslow Road that those working at the studio occasionally used. This particular night was one of the rare occasions, that John E. had joined Arthur Mertz and together they spent most of the evening having a quiet drink and a chat. At 10.30pm when the pub closed its doors, the pair moved into the back room. Suddenly, the back door opened and in strode a particularly lively Josef Locke. Sitting beside them, Joe tried to sell a revolver to them, thinking it may do for a prop. Politely refusing his offer, they continued chatting for about thirty minutes before the back door again opened. This time the police entered, a sergeant and a constable both in uniform. Did they arrest the threesome for after hours drinking? No. They took off their helmets, sat down and joined in the conversation. Before long, the sergeant was asking Joe to give them a song. After singing all day and all night, Joe declined the invitation. The sergeant however, continually pestered him until he finally succumbed and agreed to sing one song. Unfortunately, once Joe had started, it seems he didn't know when to stop. Having virtually begged him to sing they were all now begging him to stop.

Perhaps one of the most loved stars that worked at Film Studios Manchester was Tessie O'Shea. Tessie made two films for Blakeley both with Randle, whom she had appeared with previously in variety. Always billed as 'Two Ton Tessie', in consequence of her size, this Cardiff born bundle of fun had made her stage debut as a twelve-year-old in Bristol. She had based her early act on the famous music hall artiste Lily Morris and indeed used many of her songs. Through the ensuing years, she gained much experience and by the late 1930s had progressed to achieve star status. During the war years, she toured with ENSA and appeared in *'Happydrome'* with Harry Korris, she also shared top billing with Max Miller at the London Palladium. Tessie returned to this famous venue in 1946 alongside Jewel and Warriss and also for a spot in the Royal Command Performance. Her popularity continued as she made many stage and radio appearances, usually singing her own comic compositions while accompanying herself on the banjoulele. Her over-the-top effervescent personality endeared her to audiences everywhere. She was eventually to find fame in the States, crossing the Atlantic in the sixties; in fact, she probably achieved more in America than she had in Britain. She was the recipient of a Tony Award for her Broadway performance in

'Ten Ton' Tessie O'Shea was the star of two Blakeley produced films

'The Girl who came to Dinner'. She also appeared in the stage production of *'How Green was my Valley'*, again on Broadway and won an Emmy Award for her performance in American Television's *'Dr Jekyll and Mr Hyde'*. She returned to Britain occasionally for stage or TV work, but eventually settled in the States where she continued with a very successful career, which latterly included an appearance in the Disney classic *'Bedknobs and Broomsticks'*. Her time at the Manchester Studio seems to have been a happy experience and it appears everyone working there liked her. Wynne Mertz described her as a lovely person, but one who she thought was very careful with her money. Wynne had finished work one Saturday at 3.00pm when almost everyone else had gone home. Having closed her office, she was on her way down the stairs when Tessie O'Shea approached her. 'Oh Darling, could you let me have a tuppence-halfpenny stamp?' asked Tessie. Wynne explained that she could, but to get it she would have to go back up stairs to open the office. Then unlock the safe and after that the box to get at the stamps, which she did. Returning, she gave the stamp to Tessie whom in turn proffered at three-penny bit. Looking in her purse Wynne realised that she didn't have a halfpenny for Tessie's change. Apologising she said she would have to go back upstairs again. To which Tessie replies, 'Oh, it's alright darling - you can give it to me on Monday'. When Monday arrived and Tessie was back in the studio filming, Wynne went along to her dressing room where David Rollo, Tessie's husband, was with colleagues of Tessie's for lunch. After telling the tale, she explained that she had brought Miss O'Shea's halfpenny as requested. In Wynne's words, *"David Rollo was pussy-struck* [stunned] *and he said, 'well I'm sure she didn't mean it', I left it with him nonetheless. None of them ever came to me to return it, or to say I shouldn't have bothered or anything like that"*.

It was a hot June day on which they completed the last scene on *'That's My Man'*, and the heat on the studio floor had been even more unbearable than usual. Consequently, when John E. shouted 'cut', the huge studio doors were hastily flung open to let in the greatly needed fresh air. An earlier scene had featured a variety of musical instruments, which were now still lying around. Josef Locke picked up a drum and started to sing as he belted out a beat on it. All the other artistes soon followed suit picking up trumpets, trombones, in fact anything of which they could get hold. With Josef Locke leading them outside through the doors, they all marched along Dickenson Road stopping the traffic as they went along. People came from everywhere onto the street to watch, crowded buses stopped with the faces of the passengers looking out against the windows. They continued parading a lengthy way up the road before turning around and marching all the way back again to the studio - all good fun and typical of the goings on at the 'Jollywood Fun Factory'. With the last scenes safely in the can, the film went into its cutting stage and it was during this time that it also underwent a title change. Now as *'Somewhere in Politics'*, the film became the first of this series to be shot in Manchester. Happy with the completed version of the film, Mancunian arranged for it to be trade shown on 19th November 1948. It was around this same period that the two previously mentioned documentaries *'International Circus Review'* and *'Showground of the North'* also had their trade showings.

With *'Somewhere in Politics'*, completed Blakeley not only had plans to film *'The Girl at the High School'*, but had also formulated ideas for another two future productions. One of which was to deal with life in the army, a popular subject for Blakeley as he had dealt with on several previous occasions. A number of titles were being suggested for this including *'Shoulder Arms'* and *'New Army'*. Always on the lookout for talent, the summer of 1948 saw Blakeley once again taking in the holiday shows. Blackpool's season saw more than a dozen shows in town and John E. saw them all. Josef Locke, appearing at the resort with the popular comedians Jewell and Warriss steered Blakeley in their direction. Already popular through their work on BBC radio, Blakeley was obviously aware of their comic achievements. But would they be interested in film work? After seeing their performance, he approached them with his idea. Ben Warriss recalled in a Channel 4 television documentary, broadcast shortly after his death in 1993: *"My first impression of John was meeting him at the back of the stalls. "He had come to see us about doing a film and we were very keen about this. "We'd heard that he did some very good comedy films. "We'd never met the man before but knew his associate Jimmy Brennan who lived in Blackpool".* Although the duo were keen to appear in a Blakeley picture, they had to wait before making their debut in front of the cameras. For although John E. had since opening his studio completed three features, the British film industry during this time found itself in turmoil. Now in 1948, this turmoil was reaching a climax. Shortly after Blakeley had opened his studio, the British government had placed a 75% ad valorem tax on all American films coming into the country after August of 1947. As a consequence of this tax, the American film industry decided against releasing their products to the UK. With no new American films at all to screen, the British cinemas were forced into showing reissues, as not enough new British films were being produced. This resulted in the government revoking their imposed tax in May 1948. Instead, they decided that the Americans would take less of their profits out of the country reinvesting the surplus in to American backed British made products. Six months later in October 1948, a 45% quota was introduced, which compelled all cinemas in to taking that percentage of British films. This then, not only put demands on the cinemas, but even bigger burdens on the studios that simply did not have the financial resources to produce the amount of films needed. From the major studios to the smaller independents, these effects were being felt. British National collapsed in 1948, while Alexander Korda's British Lion was known to be foundering. Rank was tightening his purse strings and closures for him were just around the corner. Many studios were to remain dark and inactive all of which resulted in sizeable unemployment for many technicians and studio hands. With fewer and fewer jobs being available for the ever-increasing number of jobless, panic in the industry soon set in and they therefore called for further action from the government. Again, they tried to address the situation and by October of 1948 had announced plans for the National Film Finance Corporation to come into operation. This government-backed department immediately lent Korda's British Lion £3 million. By the time they were advancing loans to other producers whom they thought had safe sounding proposals for films, a total of seventeen studios had fallen silent, including John E. Blakeley's Film Studios (Manchester) Ltd. There was also reported to be more than a third of the 'film technicians' union members' out of work. Blakeley, himself made an approach to the NFFC, who were satisfied that his proposal had the commercial potential required. He was granted a loan of £60,000 secured against the assets and property of the Mancunian Film Corporation and the collateral security on the assets of Film Studios (Manchester) Ltd.

Financially secure Blakeley could now offer a lifeline to several members of an industry, which, to all intents and purposes, was falling apart. People, whom under normal circumstances would perhaps not have chosen to work in Manchester, began filling many of the positions offered by Blakeley. Cinematographer, Ernie Palmer was back again with the operator 'Al Britten. Also happy to be in employment were Mickey Hobbs, sound recordist and Eric Reid, boom operator, both coming from the now closed Gainsborough studio. Within the first weeks of filming, the studio's Visatone sound system began developing so many faults that production was constantly halted. John E. had also dispensed with the services of his 'head of sound and second unit recordist'. He knew though, the replacement he wanted. This was Ron Pegler, a sound recordist who had vast knowledge of the Visatone system, having worked on its initial design. Ron Pegler recalled, *"That system is what got me my job there. "Although I'd been involved in its design, I had in fact nothing to do with the mechanics and that was its Achilles tendon. "It wasn't long however, before we had to change over to the British Acoustic Film System.*"In those days it was usual practice for technicians to be employed for the duration of the film, Ron Pegler though, had managed to negotiate a twelve-month contract with Blakeley. This was at a reduced rate but it did nonetheless give him a full year of work and security at a time when the business was anything but. *"I was glad of that"*, Ron said, *"The industry was on its last legs, there was a blind panic with people falling over themselves to get jobs."Like most in Blakeley's studio I was happy to be there and in work".*

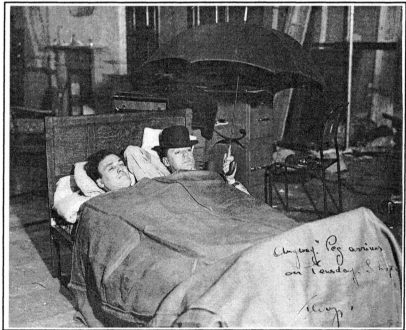

Awaiting the arrival of Ron Pegler, Terry Cotter (recordist-right) and Bob Moss (camera crew) take it easy. Terry inscribed the photo with the words 'Never mind, 'Peg' arrives on Tuesday – I hope!'

Another person thankful to John E. for employment was sixteen-year-old David Wood. David had not been employed through possessing any technical ability, for he had none, but had been given the job solely through the kindness of John E Blakeley. Joe Gomersall had been an associate of David's father, who unfortunately had died at an early age. Due to this relationship and through his own with Gomersall, John E. promised that David would have employment with him for as long as he had a studio. David Wood was taken on as clapper loader, later moving on to assistant camera operator working under John Blakeley Jnr. This had not been the first time John E. had revealed his caring nature towards a parentless youth. Several years previously he had practically semi-adopted a young pilot whose parents had lost their lives during the war. Unfortunately, the young man himself also died at an early age. Both these circumstances showed a side to John E's nature that not many people were aware of. There were other occasions too, when John E's generosity was bestowed on others. He had, at his own expense, helped to put several young men through seminary to train for the priesthood. Of course, John E, was also spurred on in this direction by his own religious convictions. Indeed the Catholic Church itself was on many occasions the beneficiary of his kindness as he paid for many churches to be painted or have minor repairs carried-out.

It was to be April 1949 when the Jewell and Warriss film went into production under the working-title of 'Somewhere on Parade'. Not only was the title a throwback to the earlier 'Somewhere' films, so too was the whole scenario. Here Jewell and Warriss were fundamentally brought in to take on roles that could easily have been played by Frank Randle and Dan Young. All the old army routines were featured including fun in the recruiting office, guard duties and the inevitable shambles with parade drill. The pair did manage to bring some of their own style and individuality to these formulaic routines, though perhaps not as much as they would have liked. During the 1970s, whilst filming an episode of 'Nearest and Dearest' we interviewed Jimmy Jewell for an intended article on Laurel and Hardy, during which the subject of John E. Blakeley came up. Jimmy recalled: *"When we arrived at the studio we had our own thoughts on how things would be. We had grown up watching the likes of Laurel and Hardy and later Abbott and Costello. Our expectations were based on this type of filmed comedy, but that's not how it turned out. I suppose because here in Britain we don't seem able to make it work on film. John Blakeley had his own way of working and we had our own*

94

Crew and cast on 'Somewhere on Parade' (What-a-Carry-On!) 1949 - Front row (left) John Blakeley jnr, Tom Blakeley, Dot Stimson. Actors Shirley Quentin, Anthony Oakley and Terry Randall, John E. Blakeley, (unknown), Ernie Palmer, (unknown). Behind and right of John E. is Bud Kelly. Extreme right of picture (standing) is Gerry Varney 'head electrician'. Extreme left (standing) is Jimmy Woods 'sound camera operator', just visible above him is Ron Pegler. While Eric Read the boom swinger is leaning on the boom. Between Tom Blakeley and Dot Stimson is Mickey Hobbs. To the right of the clapperboard is David Wood.

95

ideas, and we often disagreed. We would have liked it if he'd done things our way but he never gave in. This did cause some friction between us, and because we had our own thoughts people often thought that at times we were trying to take over. For example, look at Laurel and Hardy. How Ollie would turn to the camera and in close-up would give that famous look of exasperation at Stan. That's the kind of thing that we wanted to put across but Blakeley didn't want any of that, he just wanted us there in front of camera, no fancy close-ups or anything. Don't get me wrong, even though we had some disagreements we really did enjoy making the films, it was a marvellous time". The film also starred Shirley Quentin, Tony Pendrell, Terry Randall and appearing in what was the last of his three Blakeley films Josef Locke. Billed as the 'Celebrated Irish Tenor' not only was he given the opportunity to sing - belting out with gusto the popular 'Le Reve Passe' (The Soldier's Dream) and the more sacred 'Ave Maria' and 'Abide With Me' - but also to show that he had now become a more than competent actor. From the outset of the studio opening, the sound department had continually been hampered with the building's acoustics, and things had been no better on this production. Ron Pegler had arrived during the shooting and knew clearly, what was causing the problems. He recalled, "When I first arrived I found the number one stage was really too dead for music recordings. We tried livening it up by putting flats up against the walls and even using reverb mikes, but that didn't work very well. "The number two stage, had a very bad flutter echo in the clerestory. We managed to put a whole load more acoustic mattresses up there and kill that to some extent, but the sound insulation of the roof wasn't very good on that stage, and if any heavy lorry went past on the road, it was liable to mess up the take". With filming of 'Somewhere on Parade' completed on 24th May 1949 it moved as usual into the cutting stage, here it also went under a title change, becoming 'What-a-Carry On!'.

Free Admission ticket for the Trade Show of "What-A-Carry-On" at the Deansgate Theatre, Manchester, Friday August 26ᵗʰ 1949.

Within a matter of a few weeks the studio was busy once again as *'School for Randle'* - the new name for *'The Girl at the High School'* - began its shoot. Ernie Palmer, having already worked on the previous two Blakeley films, was again engaged as cinematographer on *'School for Randle'*. The studio in fact was fast becoming like home for Ernie, as he was to work on all, except one, of the future Blakeley productions. Again, Al Britten was the operator on first camera, with Cyril Gray as focus puller. John Blakeley Junior was on second camera with Ronnie Maasz on focus. The new found title of the film was apt, as Randle played the part of 'Flatfoot' Mason, janitor at Lyndhurst High School. Dan Young and Alec Pleon as Clarence and 'Blockhead' respectively, helped him in his duties. Flatfoot has a daughter, Betty (Terry Randall) a pupil at the school. Betty though, is unaware of this situation, believing her adoptive parents to be her real mother and father. Randle is given plenty of opportunity to show off a different side to his usual character in acting out the role of a caring father figure. In continually looking out for Betty's welfare, the two become close. Their familiarity, compounded by Betty's regular visits to Flatfoot's boiler-house sanctum, are misconstrued by the school authorities. Flatfoot is advised, if only for appearances sake, to end the relationship, something which he reluctantly agrees to. Betty, who has been nurturing a desire to work in variety, a yearning strongly opposed by her parents, decides to run away to join a theatre company. Flatfoot, who himself had been a music hall artiste has an inclination where she may be and along with Clarence and Blockhead set off in pursuit. The threesome eventually tracks her down to a low-grade theatre. Their only means of entering however, is by dressing up as a Chinese Speciality Act. This of course gives the trio plenty of opportunity for some slapstick tomfoolery and lands them on stage where as the 'Three Who Flungs' perform a comedy magic routine. Flatfoot eventually manages to speak to Betty and persuades her to return home, where she introduces Flatfoot to her parents. Realising who he really is the truth is revealed, but everyone agrees that things should remain as they are. The film ends on a high as Betty along with her friend Ted (John Singer), both having been coached by Flatfoot, win a swimming competition for the school. Location shots for the swimming sequences were undertaken at the Sale Lido. The arrangements were made for a one-day shoot and all was going to plan until everyone returned from lunch. Several crewmembers had that day opted for a 'liquid lunch' and Ernie Palmer obviously having overindulged came staggering back to the poolside. Hanging on to one of the lighting stands, he managed to send it splashing into the water. Not a clever thing to do especially as they were using high voltage. This incident didn't go down very well with John E. who was forced to send everyone home. This made for a second day's filming at the Lido and another day in which John E. was non-to pleased. On this occasion John Blakeley Jnr. always having had aspirations for the main camera persuaded his father to let him film a sequence from the Lido scheduled for the first camera. The scene, which young John was to film, involved Randle fooling around on a diving board thirty feet above the pool. He was then to capture Randle's 'accidental' fall from the board into the water below. Regrettably, John was much too slow in reacting to Randle's rapid descent and was unable to keep him in frame. Ronnie Maasz as John's focus puller recalled the outcome: *"When John E. asked his son how the shot had gone, John Junior shuffled his feet. 'Come on what happened', his father asked. 'Well er... er... dad, he left me with an empty picture'. "John E. regarded his son for a moment, aware that his junior offspring had done it again. "John E. declared it's no good we shall have to send for 'Al [Britten]. "Send for 'Al they did and poor John Junior once again was relegated".*

David Wood, clapper loader on 'School for Randle' at the Sale Lido

'*School for Randle*' also featured appearances by Jimmy Clitheroe, Gus Aubrey and Maudie Edwards, the Welsh comedienne and singer. The 4foot 2inch Clitheroe had been in show business for many years and although originally appearing in variety as a musical accordionist it was as the diminutive cheeky schoolboy that gained him his popularity. It was with the 'schoolboy' role in the BBC radio show, '*The Clitheroe Kid*' that he was to reach the pinnacle of his career. The series ran from 1955 – 1972 and with 300 episodes, being transmitted became the longest running radio sitcom on British radio.

Jimmy Clitheroe – the eternal 'schoolboy – appeared in 'Somewhere in Politics' and 'School for Randle' before achieving stardom through radio.

Before making his two appearances for Blakeley, Clitheroe had already had several other minor films roles including one with Arthur Lucan in the 'Old Mother Riley' series. Stan Little, who Blakeley had also used in two films (the earlier *'Off the Dole'* and *'Home Sweet Home'*), was an actor in similar vein to Clitheroe and both were of course, destined to spend their lives playing the eternal schoolboy.

In *'School for Randle'* there is a memorable routine involving the then 28 years-old Clitheroe, Dan Young and Frank Randle. As always, it is Frank Randle who manages to steal the scene and with the aid of a prop cow delivers some amusing dialogue.

Randle (to pupils): *"A little lecture on the cow. "The cow is used by farmers to eat grass and a cow's husband is called a b-hull [bull]. To be able to distinguish a bull from a cow, offer it a handful of hay. If she comes for it, it's a cow. If he comes for it run like He[ll] ...the very Devil. "Now from the cow we get Cowheels, Cowslips and Cow-cumbers, and sometimes we get milk. If their tails get frostbitten, we get ice cream. Now you will see the cow is a very large animal, but not quite as large as a bigger one of the same size. The cow has a leg at each corner and several other appendages that we need not go into at the moment."*

Maudie Edwards, who hailed from Neath, played the part of Bella Donna the school cook. This popular Welsh artiste actually only featured in two scenes, one a kitchen slapstick sketch with Dan Young and Alec Pleon. The other alongside Randle and Jimmy Clitheroe, in which she makes a move for Randle, who contradictory to his usual character actually rebuffs her advances. Maudie Edwards who at one time had her own Swansea based group of theatrical players, soon became a favourite in both Wales and England appearing in many stage revues. Her film work spanned over thirty years in which she appeared with many notable names the likes of Will Hay, Googie Withers, Peter Sellers, Sian Phillips and Peter O'Toole. During 1950, she appeared with Frank Sinatra - making his first British visit - for the duration of his London Palladium run. Another interesting fact in Maudie's career was that she had the distinction of speaking the initial words in the very first episode of Granada Television's *'Coronation Street'*. She played the part of Elsie Lappin, original owner of the corner shop, which she was in the process of selling to Florrie Lindley. Although her part in *'School for Randle'* was not a major one, she did also appear in what may well have been an out-take from the film, the

100

'School for Randle'. - Front Row (left) Ronnie Maasz. Cyril Gray. David Wood. Second Row (left) Dot Stimson. Eric Read. Mickey Hobbs. Doris Martin. John E. Blakeley. Tom Blakeley. Frank Randle. Ernie Palmer. Bud Kelly. Third Row (left) with arms folded is Arthur Mertz. Behind John E. is Mary Waller (striped dress) with her sister to her right.

seventeen-minute short 'Bella's Birthday'. The indications that the content of 'Bella's Birthday' were actually intended for inclusion in the full-length feature are that Edwards, Randle, Young and Pleon all play the same characters. Also, virtually the whole of the two-reeler is of musical content in similar vein to the obligatory Blakeley inserted musical concerts of old. Nevertheless, it is a fact that the footage was never to appear in the completed 'School for Randle'. Mike Blakeley indicates that 'Bella's Birthday' was shot rather quickly, over a weekend; due to the fact, that Maudie Edwards' contract was about to run out. It is also interesting to note that the film's credits acknowledge Tom Blakeley, rather than his father John E. as Producer and Director. Void of a story, other than visiting a public house to celebrate Bella's birthday, this short gives an opportunity for the stars to show their musical talent. First up is Alec Pleon, who performs one of his own compositions complete with all his usual face contorting expertise. Next, was Maudie Edwards, who as Bella Donna, sings the song 'Movie Queen'. Frank Randle, as a rather inebriated Flatfoot, subsequently takes to the stage; though, as he puts it, not before having a little more "tonsil varnish". Randle gives a rather intoxicated and highly amusing interpretation of 'Sweet and Low'. Dan Young, however, refrains from singing, opting instead to give a rendition on the violin of 'I'll Take You Home Again Kathleen'. Amidst the applause of the pub's regulars the camera pulls back to reveal musician Tommy Whitefoot actually performing the number. This then was the sum of 'Bella's Birthday', released to the cinemas in the late summer of 1950. Tommy Whitefoot was the business partner of Billy Butler, who had taken over from Fred Harris as the studio Musical Director. It appears that Harris may have been replaced after some sort of confrontation with Frank Randle. Ron Pegler recalled, *"Whitefoot always said what a fortunate place Manchester was to work in, because he could scratch around and get a fairly good orchestra together at a few hours notice".* He continued, *"Because of the acoustical problems surrounding the recording of music at the studio, it was decided that the music for 'School for Randle' would be performed and recorded at a cinema at Sale".*

When shooting on 'School for Randle' ended on 25th August 1949 the studio fell silent and remained so until January 1950 when 'Over the Garden Wall' went into production. The title for this film was taken from a sketch made famous in the theatres and on national radio by Rochdale comedian Norman Evans (see Appendix 2:4). Although Blakeley used music-hall stars and the characters they created, this was

102

the first time he had basically built a whole film around such a character. It was Norman Evans' only visit to the Rusholme studio and throughout the film he appeared in drag, portraying his characterisation of a northern housewife. Although Evans was quite well known, he did not command the same wages as Locke or Randle. He earned around £750 a week, of which £50 was paid to him in cash for his immediate needs with the remainder being paid by cheque. Everyone working at the studio got on well with Norman and Wynne Mertz thought him the perfect gentleman. Each week when in receipt of his fifty pounds he would offer Wynne a five-pound note to buy herself some nylons. She would always refuse indicating to him that she was already paid well enough. Nonetheless, he would insist, as he said he wanted to give her 'a little bit of a treat', as he was grateful for all she did. 'Over the Garden Wall' also starred Jimmy James (real name James Casey), famed in variety for his drunken routine. This he performed aided by just one prop, a broken cigarette that hung from his mouth, his facial expressions had audiences everywhere laughing. Two gormless stooges, Hutton Conyers and Bretton Woods, would always assist Jimmy James in his stage act. Conyers and Woods were just stage names and over the years, various people played the parts. Originally James' brother-in-law, Jack Derby, had played Conyers followed by his son James Casey Jnr.; later Roy Castle also performed the role. Conyers had a saying, which soon became his catchphrase 'Are you puttin' it about that I'm barmy'. James' nephew, Jack Casey played the role of Bretton Woods, later becoming Eli Woods. In actual fact, the famous line uttered by Conyers was, in the film, delivered instead by fellow stooge Eli Woods. While filming in Manchester the members of the Casey family, Jimmy James, son James (Jimmy), brother Peter (his dresser) and Eli Woods (Jack Casey his nephew) all shared the same digs. It was at their digs that James asked his son Jimmy Casey if he would write a few comic lines for him and Norman Evans to use in the following morning's shoot. Jimmy Casey, later that night spent time alone in his room and before long had written something he thought suitable for Evans and his dad. The following day Blakeley stood and read Casey's work, 'Aye lad very funny but that's London comedy' was his remark. Jimmy James, who was in his son's words "a talking comedian" asked 'what's wrong, what did Blakeley mean?' His son informed him that he meant it was dialogue, it was sentences - you're not falling over, he explained.

103

One day while James was on set filming, Peter Casey, Jimmy Casey, and Eli Woods were sitting together on a skip in the dressing room playing cards. Wynne Mertz entered the room to pay James his wage, which at around £500 was somewhat less than that of some of the other stars. The group of card players told her that he was filming but that she could leave his salary with them and they would sort it out. Wynne refused their offer, especially as Jimmy James needed to sign for it. Later, on the set, James duly signed for his money and promptly told Wynne to 'take it back to the lads and tell 'em to save me a bit'. They were of course honest and it never bothered James that they were taking their money from his wage. Wynne often heard them saying 'now that's the boss's' as they put some money to one side. Although James was renowned for playing a drunken character, he himself never drank alcohol. On stage or on set it was always cold tea when alcohol was required. In *'Over the Garden Wall'* James played the part of Joe Lawton, drunken husband of Fanny (Norman Evans). They receive a telegram informing them their daughter's return from America for a visit. When she arrives, she meets up with an old boyfriend and although they are both married, an affair seems to be in the offing. This poses problems, as the boyfriend is the son of James' boss. Of course, when their partners find out, they nip things in the bud. The script caused quite a commotion on the set as it called for the daughter to bring her baby back with her from the States. No one knew though if the baby was supposed to be a boy or a girl, the screenplay just said 'baby'. Finally, Blakeley had to be consulted and he informed everyone that 'baby' was in fact the name of a dog. This left everyone thinking the same thought, 'where to get a dog'. As it happened, Dot Stimson was in digs where a Samoyed had just given birth to six or seven pups. She took one of these along with her to the studio and when John E. saw the pup he knew that it was what he wanted. The pup, which she had intended to be her own, was to become a star. After a couple of weeks she wanted to take the pup home agreeing to bring in another as a sort of stand-in. She finished taking all the pups in at varying stages, one by one, they all appeared in the film, and no one could tell the difference. Dot Stimson sold each of them onto the artistes after filming had been completed. Quite often, when shooting, a set would not be ready and a new sequence would have to be thought up to fill the required screen time. Ronnie Maasz working again alongside Ernie Palmer recalls one such moment on *'Over the Garden Wall'*. *"There was another unfinished set on the next stage which consisted of a flight of stairs leading nowhere."* *"There was nothing in the* script about a flight of stairs but the time must not be wasted, so the cast of comics were summoned."When moving onto this set Blakeley gave out his immortal lines 'go on lads be funny'. So, a short routine was quickly put together, which involved James' late arrival home after a night out at the pub. Under the influence of the drink James was chased up and down the stairs by his wife (Norman Evans), during which time, he subsequently lost his false teeth. It was nothing much, but great play was made of it, much to the delight of Blakeley. Given the opportunity, Blakeley would whenever possible, try to save money on his productions. One scene in 'Over the Garden Wall' was filmed at Manchester's Belle Vue Ballroom. Rather than hire the venue and recruit the necessary extras, Blakeley came up with a cheeky money saving idea. He hired the ballroom, and then announced that the proposed shoot would be open to the public as a 'Grand Film Ball'. 'Come and see your favourite stars making their latest film proclaimed the advertisements, payment on entry! Come along they did, in droves, ensuring Blakeley had recouped a substantial part of the hire charge. Ron Pegler recalled, *"It didn't quite work out the way he expected though. For he almost had a revolt on his hands, as the paying public objected strongly to being herded about and shouted at by the megaphone wielding John Blakeley. "They quite rightly thought they had been cheated, he really did have a nerve".*

'Over the Garden Wall' had its trade showing during April 1950 going on release during the summer. This general release did not however, include showings at the Rank cinemas. As with all cinemas at the time, the Rank Circuit was compelled by the government to take a 30% quota of British films. In spite of this, in the year 1949-50 Rank failed to meet this criterion, as the company was unable to find enough home produced products to screen. They rejected eleven films as unsuitable for playing as first features without the fear of actually losing money. Out of these eleven films, three were the Blakeley productions, *'What-a-Carry On!'*, *'School for Randle'* and *'Over the Garden Wall'*. Blakeley of course, was not surprised by Rank's attitude, as the major cinemas had never truly taken any of his previous films for a circuit release. This situation was something that continually annoyed and irked him, much in the same way, as the London critics did. Perhaps the bad review for *'School for Randle'* caused Blakeley to hit back, when he spoke out against certain critics; *"How can anyone in London judge a film of mine when they don't know the first thing about the people for whom I cater? "It's hard work battling with critics. It's bad enough competing with US films without being hampered by slams from reviewers"*. On the trade advertising for *'School for Randle'*, aimed at cinema proprietors he took matters a step further, by proclaiming in large letters 'DON'T RELY ON PRESS REPORTS'. Notwithstanding the critics, or lack of a circuit release, *'What-a-Carry On!'*, *'School for Randle'*, and *'Over the Garden Wall'*, all managed to turn a profit. It was with thanks to the numbers of independent cinemas that this was accomplished, and although not vast, it was a profit nonetheless.

Having vented his spleen at the critics, Blakeley put their comments behind him. For almost ten years, they had never really had a good word for him, so why should he let them get the better of him now. Spurred on, he turned to what he could do best; making pictures. Blakeley's next film *'Let's have a Murder'*, went into production around March 1950. This film saw the return to the Rusholme studio of radio comics Jimmy Jewell and Ben Warriss. *'Let's have a Murder'* had a story written by Anthony Toner and was adapted for the screen by Harry Jackson and Robert Taylor. The comic duo play the parts of Warren and Jewsbury, bumbling detectives who are offered a £10,000 fee to clear the name of their client's son, who it transpires, has been arrested for murder. According to critics of the time *'Let's have a Murder'*, with a running time of around 108minutes, could have been improved through thoughtful cutting. Unfortunately, *'Let's have a Murder'* is today one of the 'lost' Mancunian Films. Surviving however, is the shortened fifty-minute reissue version titled *'Stick 'Em Up'* which was released in 1959. This version does manage to retain the main storyline and the closing-up of the action makes it quite enjoyable viewing. The twosome certainly seem to come across better than in their previous film, probably as their roles are essential to the story and every comic situation furthers this along. Their funny routines and comic patter seem to be well structured and remain within the confines of the story as opposed to the isolated routines in *'What-a-Carry-On!'*. Their skill is brought to the fore in an excellent ghostly cellar scene and their versatility is shown when Jimmy dons drag on more than one occasion, all to good effect.

The arrangement that had been made between the NFFC and the Mancunian Film Corporation was that the repayment of the loan was to have been made by June 1950. The NFFC however, had deferred payment until January 1951. Nonetheless, Blakeley had actually started making repayments during September of 1950. Now, with the January deadline approaching it was evident that a final payment

106

would leave Mancunian, with no funds to finance a new picture, and the prospect of the permanent closure of the studio. Blakeley's dilemma was a simple one. The money available to him could be used either to finance a film or to pay off the loan, but not both. The solution was not to be so simple. Consequently, he arranged a meeting between himself and the NFFC at which he asked for the possibility of another deferment or even of an additional loan. The outcome, according to Blakeley was that not only did the NFFC refuse to accommodate him but that they were also indifferent as to the fate of the studio, even threatening to send in the receivers to secure their money. John E. also formed the impression that had they known the type of film he was producing he would not even have been granted the original loan. That same day he met with film editor Dot Stimson at London's Trocodero Restaurant, Shaftsbury Avenue. Dot said, *"He was absolutely devastated at the news, he just couldn't believe it"*, *"He also*

The sound crew on 'Let's Have a Murder'. Top (left) Jimmy Wood. Micky Hobbs. Front (left) David Wood. Lesley Osmond (actress) 'Hairdresser' and member of camera crew. Standing to the rear of David Wood is Ron Pegler.

February 1950 –
John E. Blakeley ploughs through his books while still wearing
his 'trademark' homburg hat

told me that he thought another reason he'd been turned down was because he'd made four films with the money they'd loaned him for three. The NFFC though contended that their threat to appoint a receiver had only been made when Blakeley suggested that he might repay loans due to his company's directors before discharging his debt to them. The Corporation also refuted Blakeley's view that they would not have given him a loan if they had known the type of film he was producing. Their position was that they did not judge standards of films. They based their decisions solely on a film's drawing power with the cinema-going public. The NFFC claimed that Blakeley's own estimates for the films made with money from the loan had fallen drastically. This indicated to them that the public no longer wanted to see Blakeley's films. Consequently, they could see no reason why further films should be made with money due to the corporation. Blakeley finally accepted that the repayment would have to be made and it was completed by May 1951.

Chapter Five

It was now crisis time at Film Studios Manchester. With the outlook rather grim, a meeting of the directors was called to decide the future of the studio. Tom was convinced that the way forward was with 'light' comedies, which at this time were very popular. Perhaps his biggest hurdle though, was not in convincing backers that they could produce such pictures, which indeed would have to be done, but in trying to persuade his father. John E. on the other hand was still convinced that his kind of pictures could still prove popular. No immediate decision was reached and over the next few months, much deliberating took place. Finally, a plan for the studios future was put together. It was decided that the studio itself would be hired out to anyone who wished to use its facilities, something that would bring in funds while they gradually carried out the rest of their plan. Several stage plays were viewed, and scripts studied from which they were to choose three that were suitable for adaptation for the screen. These, they hoped optimistically, would attract new investors for this type of production. Nonetheless, it also appears that the studio directors themselves may have all had to dig deep into their own pockets to help put their plan into being. Eventually, a number of plays were chosen which they thought would make ideal light comedy films. H.F. Maltby, an actor and playwright who had appeared in Blakeley's production of '*Home Sweet Home*', had written three of those selected. He had also been invited to write a screenplay for an army comedy burlesque, which John E. thought he could make into a success. By September 1951 their plans were put into action when James Carreras's Exclusive/Hammer company moved into the studio to film '*Never Look Back*'. It appears that Jimmy Brennan, one of the main directors of the studio, was the one responsible for bringing the Carreras production to Manchester. Whether Brennan's help with the film's finance had any bearing on the deal being realised is unclear, though, this was something he did in fact do. The film's director, Francis Searle told us, *"The first thing that shook me when I arrived in Manchester was Jimmy Brennan. I don't know whether he was the moneybags or what. But he seemed so. "When I got up there, there was a big Rolls Royce for me to use all the time. I was staying at the Midland Hotel, which was nice, but I didn't want this Rolls Royce picking me up, especially as I was on my own. So eventually they got me a somewhat less ostentatious vehicle". "The whole thing had been organised by Brennan.* Jimmy Brennan also received a co-producer credit along with Michael Carreras on the film, which was something else that quite

109

irritated Frank Searle. *"I recall I made a complaint about that"*, explained Frank, *"...for to have coupled Brennan with Carreras just wasn't fair. "Jimmy Brennan had absolutely nothing whatsoever to do with the production side at all, and even Michael rode in on my back, being the son of Jim Carreras. "I myself had actually worked on the script with the writer and technically produced the thing. "I suppose thinking about it now, if Jimmy Brennan was a 'money man' and had put up a substantial amount of cash then I suppose technically he could also be classed as co-producer. "However, I nearly fell apart when I saw Jimmy Brennan's name. "I had also worked on the script and received a co-script credit. Of course it's with the preparation of the script where a lot of the producing goes"*. Having worked at many London studios throughout his career, Frank didn't find the Manchester studio too bad of a place to work. *"It was a jolly nice studio really, but it wouldn't compare even to say Riverside or Southall. "I do know that with the small stage at Rusholme, I only just managed to squeeze in the Old Bailey set. Which I'd had sent up on low loaders from Pinewood or Elstree, or wherever it was. "Nonetheless, it certainly wasn't the worst studio that I'd worked in, not by a long way"*.

Tom Blakeley, who had the nominal role of Assistant Producer on 'Never Look Back', was one day chatting on the set with his father and visitor Robert Stead. Robert, who was Head of BBC programmes in the North, knowing the difficulty and problems at the studio, made the remark about the possibility of the BBC hiring or even buying the studio. Television, as he put it, was driving northwards and there was neither time nor enough money to build provincial studios. Nothing however, was to materialise from this conversation until several years later. Nonetheless, it would have been something never far from John's thoughts, especially with the situation as it was.

As the film starring Rosamund John, Hugh Sinclair and Guy Middleton was shooting, John E. announced, that along with the H. F. Maltby plays three other productions would also be undertaken. The first *'Love's a Luxury'* was to start shooting as soon as Exclusive had vacated the studio. Quickly following this would be *'Those People Next Door'*. The third being the comedy burlesque, which was still being worked on by John E. and its screenwriter H.F. Maltby. While it was appropriate that John E. would be in charge of this production he was however, to leave *'Love's a Luxury'* and *'Those People Next Door'* in the hands of others more suited to light comedy. Tom Blakeley, now as producer, brought Francis Searle back to Manchester for the first production. Frank said, *"I think they wanted someone more suited to working with film actors rather than music hall artistes. "I don't for a moment want to decry dear old John E; he was of a different school and techniques change as they have many times since. "I know his directorial procedure were somewhat different and dear old John used to get his people together and I believe all he used to say was 'go on be funny'. "I didn't actually have a great deal to do with him, though he did use to come on the set occasionally."*

When Francis Searle first saw a scenario for Guy Paxton and Edward V. Hoile's play *'Love's a Luxury'*, he was surprised to find that it had not been adapted ready for the screen. Enlisting the services of scriptwriting friend Elwyn Ambrose, the two of them cut out masses of dialogue. Frank again recalled, *"It was much too wordy and as a play had too many scenes where they ended with a fade out to black, which was no good to us"*. The star of the film, Hugh Wakefield, for some reason also seems to have achieved a co-credit as scriptwriter, something that baffled Francis Searle. Also starring along side Wakefield in *'Love's a Luxury'* was Derek Bond, Michael Medwin, Helen Shingler, Zena Marshall and Patricia Raine, with Bill Shine and Grace Arnold. The story has Charles Pentwick (Wakefield) as the leader of a company of local actors, who, having squabbled with his rather reserved wife, heads off to a country retreat. With him is one of his leading players, Robert Bentley (Bond). Young and attractive Molly Harris (Raine), the caretaker's daughter, is running the hotel with help from her mother (Arnold). The arrival of Mrs Pentwick (Shingler) accompanied by her son (Medwin) and his girlfriend (Marshall) marks the start of some comic complications. Including, bizarre disguises, phoney policemen and a crazy scoutmaster and group of scouts encamped in the grounds.

As a film director Searle had been used to working with uncomplicated sets, those that offered ease of movement, or could be effortlessly disassembled. He was soon to discover that Joe Gomersall's sets were the complete opposite. He recalled, *"One big problem was the so-called art director, who with respect to him, was not so much an art director as a builder. "He made everything solid. I couldn't get the camera dollies through the doors and that sort of thing"*. Of the rest of the studio crew Frank said, *"I think when they got the idea that we were making a different kind of movie it got people a bit more on their toes. I remember the editor Dot Stimson; I got on very well with her. Perhaps for her, cutting a film like this was a bit different from all the usual static stuff she was used too"*. Most of the shooting had taken place at the studio, but there were also several location scenes, one of which called for an olde worlde looking cottage. A cottage was

111

eventually found complete with old oak beams, but before the camera started rolling, it was decided that it didn't look quite right. Apparently, it was to clean. It looked almost new. Indeed, it looked too much like a film set. What followed could have easily been an excerpt from one of John E's, films. In making the cottage more weather beaten and rustic, most of the crew ended up running around throwing buckets of muddy water at the walls.

While *'Love's a Luxury'* was going through its postproduction stages during February 1952, filming was already underway on *'Those People Next Door'*. This was the new title for *'Wearing the Pants'*, a play written by Zelda Davees. Described as a pleasant unassuming little comedy, Tom was hoping to complete the shooting on a budget of £50,000. The film was to be directed by John Harlow, whose earlier work included several 'Old Mother Riley' comedies.

Much of the action to the film took place at number six Bagthorpe Street in the imaginary town of Kimsley. Heading the cast was Jack Warner, who had appeared by permission of the J. Arthur Rank Organisation. When first offered the role of Sam Twigg, the head of a typical wartime English provincial family, Warner had had misgivings. He had been aware of the studio methods of filmmaking. The happy-go-lucky way in which they produced their comedies, while being successful, was not one he wanted to risk his reputation on. With this in mind, he first insisted that he receive a script. In addition, he informed them that he had no desire to stray from his ordinary Cockney accent. *"I wasn't going to try any phoney 'Ee-Bye-Gum' dialect on Lancashire ears"*, he said at the time. His character, he advised them, must be one that had married into a Lancashire family. Playing other members of the Twigg household were, Marjorie Rhodes as his wife Mary, with Patricia Cutts, Norma Gaussons and Anthony Newley as the children. At only 22 years of age young Newley had already put a string of screen credits behind him, most notably as the Artful Dodger in the 1951 production of *'Oliver Twist'*. He had also already appeared with Jack Warner in the film *'Vote for Huggett'*. Jack Warner in his biography recounted one vivid memory of *'Those People Next Door'*. The Rusholme studio he explained was no different to any other when actors and actresses were not actually on set filming. The actors, while awaiting their call were all at a loose end with little to do. Many would pass the time playing cards while some of the females would be

112

No phoney 'ee-bye-gum' Lancashire accent for Cockney Jack Warner

knitting. More often than not though, people would usually just sit around bored out of their minds consuming pots of tea or coffee. *"Not young Anthony"*, recounted Warner, *"When he wasn't wanted he eventually decided to stretch out on the floor in some studio corner and go soundly to sleep"*. Warner continued to say of Newley that he was obviously very talented, but with the industry as it was he never imagined he would eventually reach the heights he did. Those people next door were actually neighbours Mr and Mrs Higgins played by Charles Victor and Gladys Henson. In the Twigg household Sam Twigg (Jack Warner) not only had to contend with impending air raids but also his two troublesome daughters and son Bob (Anthony Newley). The Twigg's eldest daughter Anne (Patricia Cutts) falls for the son of a titled couple, who is an officer in the RAF. Disapproving of the match, the young man's parents are about to sort things out with the Twigg's, just as their son is reported as having been shot down. When he turns up with just a broken leg, the two families are united in their joy. In some ways, the film resurrected the 'Huggett's' style of comedy, which had brought success for Jack Warner several years earlier. Garry Marsh and Peter Forbes-Robertson, and Jimmy James in his second film at the studio, all gave supporting roles. Jimmy inevitably played the part of 'the drunk'. During the evening after the first day of filming, the main cast members went along to the Playhouse in Hulme. Here they saw a performance of the play from which the film had been adapted.

'Love's a Luxury' was given its trade show on 26th September 1952 while that for *Those People Next Door'* was held during February 1953. Both films obtained good bookings guaranteeing circuit showings in over 500 cinemas. *'Love's a Luxury'* also went on to gain a good release in America under the title of *'The Caretakers Daughter'*.

Trade Advertisement

114

Although John E. had been planning to go into the studio with the comedy burlesque 'Shoulder Arms', there was to be a considerable interval before this was to be possible. Over twelve months were to pass before cameras were to start rolling again on a feature film. The main reason for the delay, again seems to have been the lack of finance. Although the studio directors had backed to a certain degree the two previous films, perhaps they were now a little wary of putting up more money. It would take at least two years before any investment could be recouped from both 'Love's a Luxury' and 'Those People Next Door' despite having both secured decent circuit bookings. Of course, with 'Shoulder Arms' being more in the vein of John E. Blakeley's previous offerings further financial backers may have been reluctant to come forward.

During this latest period of studio inactivity, one film did go into production. Produced by Tom Blakeley, 'Elephants Come to Town', filmed on location would have cost very little to produce, especially in comparison to a feature film. Shot by cameraman John Blakeley Jnr. this thirty-three minute film captured the fun of the Chipperfield's travelling circus. Edited by Dot Stimson and with a commentary by Lionel Marsden, the featurette depicted various circus acts. Complete with lions, horses, and sixteen elephants, along with acrobats and clowns. Released during April of 1953, 'Elephants Come to Town' was the ideal film for family audiences.

After the first tentative mention, whilst shooting 'Never Look Back', that the studio may be rented or bought by the BBC, during this enforced period of darkness came a more serious offer of purchase. The BBC desperately needed premises and a ready-made studio like that at Dickenson Road was ideal. They could also see that film production had over the past several years been slow and spasmodic and was now at a standstill. Indeed before 'Shoulder Arms' eventually went into production the BBC came forward again with yet another offer. John E. Blakeley obviously had to give it some thought.

Under the new title of 'It's a Grand Life', John E. started shooting on his long awaited comedy. It was now the summer of 1953 and the film's star Frank Randle had not set foot on that studio set since August 1949. Of course Randle had been kept busy with his own touring show 'Randle's Scandals' packing out northern theatres. He had also during 1950 made a television appearance and had even had aspirations of producing his own film *'Wigan Pier'*. He'd also savoured disappointment when his typical vulgar humour failed to ignite London's West End audiences during his abortive run during 1952. The London working-classes had, however, appreciated him more when he appeared in the East End shortly after. Still, to many people, by 1953 his popularity was on the wane. A strong feature film was perhaps a means of keeping him in the eye of the northern public. To this ends it also seems likely that Randle may have put more of his own money into this film.

The female star of the film was Diana Dors likened by many to a British Marilyn Monroe. Though, as she was to admit in her autobiography, (Dors, an intimate self portrait), *"An offer of £1,000 to appear in a film being made in Manchester was a far cry from Monroe's Hollywood"*. Diana had made her first film appearance (uncredited) in ' *Shop at Sly Corner'*. She played alongside Jack Warner in two of the *'Huggett'* pictures and had a spell with Rank's 'Charm School' before he closed it down. Many thought of her as just good looking and sexy, but Diana could in truth act, but was rarely given the roles to prove herself. With her appearance in *'The Weak and the Wicked'*, people did take notice and she followed this up with *'A Kid for Two Farthings'* and an excellent performance in *'Yield to the Night'*. Her aspirations were high when she moved to Hollywood. Unfortunately, she joined RKO during its own decline, the studio badly miscast her, and sadly, her American dream never materialised. She continued though, to prove a firm favourite with British audiences making many film appearances. She also had success on the small screen and starred in several shows including the sitcom *'Queenie's Castle'*, *'All our Saturdays'* and *'Just William'*. After three marriages and a career of making the headlines, Diana died in 1984. There is no doubting John E. signed up Diana Dors, on the drawing power of her looks, rather than her acting ability, indeed he bills her in the credits as 'Britain's Most Beautiful and Glamorous'. John E. also signed Winifred Atwell, a popular musical entertainer to make a guest appearance in *'It's a Grand Life'*, along with several professional wrestlers all well known at Manchester's Belle Vue. Ernie Palmer was again director of photography with Ted Warringham on main camera.

Randle's antics prevailed throughout the production, both enlivening and hindering its progress. Once during shooting the temperamental Randle was involved in an incident that actually stopped production. Part of the duties of Bert Marrotta, the assistant director was to make sure the actors were on set when needed. Time after time, Randle, and indeed some other stars had been late and Marrotta often had to call at their hotels for them. This then had been a contributing fact as to why Randle had taken a dislike to him, and was now refusing to go on set. In fact, Randle in so many words, issued an ultimatum that the assistant director had to go or he and others would not finish the film. John Blakeley, unusually bowed to his star's wishes and Bert Marrotta found himself laid off. This was a course of action that did not go down well with the rest of the technical crew. They in turn refused to work unless Blakeley reinstated Marrotta. Eventually John E. asked Bert Marrotta to come back. A total of three days were lost, because of Randle's moods. Perhaps surprisingly, after the filming of the party scene, which appears at the end of the film, Randle asked John E. to keep the cameras rolling. John E. duly obliged to his request and in front of the camera Randle went up to Bert Marrotta and shook his hand, saying how sorry he was and apologised for being an absolute bastard. On another occasion as coloured performer Winifred Atwell

John E. directs 'It's a Grand Life' as Winifred Atwell looks on

was playing the piano, Randle was to appear doing a silly little dance. Randle however, in one of his tasteless pranks thought that doing it blacked-up complete with white gloves, minstrel-like, would be funny. Fortunately John E. having got wind of this informed the crew, 'I know what he's going to do but don't worry he's not going to ruin it'. When filming began John E. put the main camera on Winifred. The number two camera, which was supposedly for Randle, was also focused on her. He then kept Randle waiting in the wings until the shot was about two-thirds through. When John E. eventually called him on, Randle proceeded with a wonderful comic dance routine. After the shot was completed, Randle was quite pleased with his prank. Winifred Atwell though, was not. To her, the whole thing was a terrible insult. She came over to Dot Stimson and said, 'had I known there were going to be two coloured artistes I wouldn't have appeared'. Still Randle thought the whole thing extremely funny and couldn't wait to see the rushes. Randle was livid when he eventually viewed them the following afternoon. For the way John E. had placed the cameras all that could be seen of Randle were his white-gloved hands flying in and out of frames, he wasn't in the main shot at all. It taught Randle a lesson for he just quietly walked out of the theatre without a word of complaint. Diana Dors was never to forget her visit to the Dickenson Road studio, writing in her autobiography she said, "...the film was an utter shambles, for Randle was mad - and usually drunk into the bargain. But, as he owned the film company, we had to put up with him shooting guns at the dressing room wall or dragging his girlfriends by the hair along the corridors". Eileen Mackleston was a receptionist who was working at the studio at this time and remembers vividly an encounter with Randle during the production. The incident started quite innocently, when one day Eileen had to refuse admission to a lady friend of Randle's. She explained to the lady that he was on the set and that while the red light was showing no one could get in. This information had to be repeated several times more before the lady indignantly left. The young woman in question though formally complained to studio manager Bud Kelly. Consequently, the following day Eileen Mackleston was summoned to his office. She ran through exactly what had taken place and what had been told to the lady; all of which satisfied Bud. Eileen recalled, "Later I was in the studio canteen with some of the lads. Suddenly Frank Randle burst in. "He looked at me while shouting at the top of his voice 'I want you'. "He was going raving mad and everyone just sat there and never moved. "He kept shouting, 'I want you'. He was effing and blinding with every other word". It was one of

Diana Dors and Frank Randle in 'It's a Grand Life'

the studio hands that had been sitting with Eileen, who managed to calm Randle down. He eventually got him to return to his dressing room, but only after several hard words had been spoken. Eileen continued, *"Shortly after this, I heard bangs - gun shots. It was Randle again. "He was firing his gun and shouting 'where is she I'm going to kill her'. "So, Arthur my husband went to see him and calm him down. Which being a bit of a drinking pal of his, he eventually managed to do".* Dorothy Stimson recalled a similar tale but whether this was a separate incident or one that followed on from that same day's events is uncertain. As it was, Dot was working late one night in her cutting room, which she often did. *"This particular night".* Said Dot, *"I suddenly heard the bang, bang, of a gun going off, and I didn't know what to think. I was obviously in a slight panic not knowing what was going on. Well I'm not sure who shouted I think it was probably one of the boys from the paint shop. He shouted 'get back, get back, its Frank he's got a gun. There he was with this Luger letting loose. "I did manage to stop him in the end, I was shouting Frank, Frank, and eventually stopped him and asked him' whatever are you doing'. "It was not one of his better days. He was shocking he used to do such outrageous things".* The antics of Frank Randle have been widely documented and within the pages of this book, many have been repeated. However, we must admit that there indeed seemed to have been two sides to the man. Most of the time, he would wear the very best of suites, his hair was always well groomed and with his teeth in place, he looked every bit the gentleman. A title he could often live up to, anyone using abusive language while ladies were present were firmly put in their place by an upstanding Randle. Many people have spoken with us and told of his generosity and kindness. At times, we found it hard to believe this could be the same man responsible for so much shocking behaviour. Without doubt, to everyone he was a comic genius but when the drink took effect or a 'mood' came over him anything could and more often did happen. Unfortunately, to this day, these are the things Randle will be remembered for, but happily, there are still a few who remember the other Randle.

In *'It's a Grand Life'* Randle, Dan Young and chums are based at the 29th Army Training Camp where he serves up a formula much the same as when he first appeared in uniform in *'Somewhere in England'*. The same disregard for authority is there for all to see, smoking on parade and talking back to his superior officers whilst Randle revels in it all. Corporal Paula Clements (Diana Dors) spends a great deal of

*John E. Blakeley instructs Frank Randle in their final film
'It's a Grand Life'. Also seen are Dan Young (extreme right)
and Gus Aubrey (extreme left).*

time trying to fend off the unpleasant advances of Sergeant-Major
O'Reilly (Michael Brennan). With the arrival however, of new recruit
Private Phil Greene (John Blythe), the Sgt-Major has unwelcome
competition for her affections. With jealousy setting-in, the Sgt-Major
tries to stop the impending romance from blossoming by attempting to
have private Greene transferred overseas. Randle, true to form, is on
hand to save the day and to bring Paula and Phil together. Amidst all
this, Randle has time to ruin a parade ground drill, impersonate a
captain, and take part in a wrestling bout. The climax to the film sees
Randle being promoted to the Rank of Sergeant-Major and Winifred
Atwell's appearance at the piano. Atwell was a 'honky-tonk' style
pianist who had become popular through her BBC radio and television

appearances. Since December of 1952, she had also had records in the country's best selling record charts.

Since the studio had opened, it had been usual practice after a film had finished shooting, for those that had come up from London to return home, while most of the locally based employees like the electricians and carpenters, would be laid-off until the start of the next production. Wynne Mertz recalled, *"Between films there was only ever a skeleton staff. I was always there during these dark spells as there was always clerical work to do"*. Therefore, when filming on *'It's a Grand Life'* had concluded, no one thought any more about it when the same practice was carried out. They would have been unaware that the completion of the Randle feature was also to bring to an end an era of feature production at the studio and indeed its ultimate closure. Wynne Mertz recalled, *"Arthur came home one day saying he thought the money had dried up and that we wouldn't be making any more films. "Shortly after that he was told he'd be finishing on a certain day"*.

The news that the studio would be closing shocked those people still in employment there, and would have completely surprised those who were hoping to return with the start of a new picture. Why then, did the studio have to cease production, especially when it had always been said that the films all made money? Of course, there are many aspects to consider when answering this question. Television at the time was becoming increasingly popular and with the televised coronation of Queen Elizabeth in June 1953 the sale of television sets soared. From this time on, television was to go from strength to strength and cinema audiences were drastically falling. John E. Blakeley was of course getting older and it was no secret that he was not a well man. A doctor had been a regular visitor on the studio set. Then there was the all important money situation; the studio certainly had cash-flow problems. John E. was later to admit, *"All the films produced at Dickenson Road made money, but not enough"*. Adding to the problems were the unsolicited offers coming from the BBC for the purchase of the studio. Putting all these things together and it seemed the fate of the studio was set.

Negotiations with the BBC were to be long and drawn out and before they reached the final agreement Blakeley hired out the studio for the filming of a commercial. All the technical staff for the shooting came up with the production company from London. The advertisement

ARTHUR ASKEY

Top grossing, film comedian Arthur Askey's only work at 'Film Studios Manchester' was confined to a toothpaste commercial.

they were to work on was one for toothpaste and was to have as its star Arthur Askey. This well-known Liverpool comedian had several years earlier appeared in a series of advertisements for 'Gibbs SR' toothpaste. Richard Massingham directed all these, under the umbrella title of 'Arthur Askey on going to the Dentist'. It cannot be said with any certainty, whether this advert was also for Gibbs SR, though, having used the star previously it seems likely. The choice of the Manchester Studios seems to have been made as a matter of convenience to the star. Having laid-off most of the staff, Blakeley did not have the services of a dresser to offer Askey. Wynne Mertz recollects, *"Lacking a wardrobe mistress or dresser John E. persuaded our cleaner, Margaret Wilsey, an elderly Irish lady to do the job and she was happy to oblige".*

To accentuate Askey's portrayal of a little boy they had dressed him in a velvet suit. The short trouser legs of which, were each adorned with a pearl button while his top carried a white ruffle. In the advert, Askey made a court appearance where he was asked in serious tones 'did you clean your teeth today?' At some point during the proceedings, one of the pearl buttons seemed to have gone astray and so they called upon Margaret Wilsey 'the dresser' to sew it back on. Margaret's actions surprised Askey. In her attempt to replace the button, and treating the star as though he was in fact a little boy, she pushed her hand up the inside of his trouser leg. Hastily he tried to retreat, but Margaret pulled him back remonstrating with him and telling him in no

123

uncertain terms to behave. Managing to extricate himself from her clutches Arthur stormed off the set leaving Margaret cursing the unruly behaviour of the 'naughty boy'. Askey made his way into Wynn Mertz's office. She recalls, *"He came hurrying in and said 'the wardrobe mistress you've got, she's trying to put her hand up my trousers to sew a button back on. I've tried to tell her that I'm a man and not a little boy. Will you come down and tell her who I am?'- So I went back down stairs with him".* Wynne and Arthur arrived back on the set to find everyone there still in uncontrollable fits of laughter at what they had seen. *"I eventually managed to convince Margaret that Arthur was indeed a man and was a famous comedian"*, said Wynne. *"She had been totally unaware of who he really was, she had actually thought him to be a little boy".* Apart from supplying the facilities, the production of this commercial had had nothing to do with Blakeley. Though, it was certainly appropriate and must have been some consolation, to have had the last performance before the camera from a popular northern comic.

Dot Stimson, like her friend Wynne Mertz, was one of the few employees still working at the studio - almost to the very end. Since filming had ended on *'It's a Grand Life'*, Dot had been busy on its editing. The film had its first trade showing in October 1953 but this did not mean that her work was done. During her last few months at the studio Dot had edited an eighteen-minute short film comprised of footage from the earlier Jewell and Warriss feature *'What-a-Carry On!'*. This film went out on release in 1953 under the title of *'Joining the Army'*. Of course, for John E. making shorts from his features was nothing new. This had been a practice he had started in 1938 with the first of his *'Music Hall Personalities'* and was to continue with a further eighteen similarly titled films. In more recent times he'd had Dot Stimson making shorts from *'School for Randle'*, which went out on release as *'Teacher's Pest'* and *'The Three Who-Flungs'*. Dot recalled, *"John always shot so much footage during a film, that we could take unused sequences and drop them into another film. Sometimes there was even enough to make a two-reel short, which could go out to the cinemas in support of a feature. We never wasted any footage".* As with the case of *'Bella's Birthday'* a two-reel short made from material shot for *'School for Randle'* but never included in the feature. When Dot's work was finally completed and it was time for her to leave, she found the task a difficult one. Dot recalled, *"When my work at the studio was over it was a strange feeling knowing I was never to return. The last train journey from Manchester to London was a sombre occasion. It was all too much. It had been part of my life for so long. "After*

124

being home in London for just a week, almost without thinking I returned to Manchester. "It was terrible. I could not get used to the truth of it all. It just did not sink in. "You know it took me three weeks before I managed to come back home properly".

By May 1954, after receiving several offers, Blakeley finally reached an agreement with the BBC for their purchase of his studio. On 27th May, this news was featured in both the Manchester Evening newspapers, and the trade press broke the news in their next editions. The BBC announced that the studios would become the first television studios outside London and would serve the whole of the BBC Northern Region. It was also at this time that Blakeley made the statement that his films had made money, but not enough. He also stated, *"When we go into production again, it will be in London".* A reminder no doubt that Blakeley had sold only the Dickenson Road property and buildings, and that he and his companies were still in the film making business. The first BBC television transmission from Dickenson Road was on 3rd July 1954 when they broadcast 'Top Town'. This programme was a forerunner of the popular 1970s show; 'It's a Knockout'. The producer of both shows was Barney Colehan who recalled that when that show went out, the studios still had the Manchester Film Studios sign outside. He also said, *"I remember seeing the name of Diana Dors on one of the dressing room doors when we took it over from the film company".*

With the sale of the Dickenson Road premises, the Blakeley family was now conducting their business from the Mancunian offices at 3 The Parsonage. Throughout its lifetime, the studio had carried out most of its business from these offices. It had been the distribution centre for most of Film Studios Manchester's products, and so it indeed remained. For, as well as distributing *'It's a Grand Life',* there was still a viable market for the old films. Just after the studio had been sold, a deal with Butcher's Films was agreed which saw Mancunian responsible for the distribution of their films in the Liverpool and Manchester areas. John E. Blakeley's two sons, along with David Wood – the man John E. had promised employment to for as long as he had a business – moved to the Parsonage. From here they mainly worked as reps pushing the films to cinemas. Most of the other technical staff, and virtually all the studio's electricians eventually took up positions with the BBC at their former workplace.

It was the summer of 1955 before cameras were rolling again on another Mancunian film. Tom Blakeley as producer and director headed the small team that was now working as the Mancunian Film Unit. With John Blakeley Jnr in charge of photography and David Wood as his assistant, the unit took advantage of Manchester's glorious weather to shoot on location a twenty-minute short. Manchester had seen ten July days of constant 80° heat, during which time the film crew put much film in the can. The short travelogue style film, aptly titled 'Lovely Weekend' followed the exploits of three young women as they enjoyed several local attractions. The girls, Jane Peters, Deirdre Clear and Marlene Nelson were seen setting off for their caravan holiday in their sports car. Scenes of their escapades were captured at the Italian Garden at Milverton Lodge Club, Victoria Park, Manchester, the pool at Mere Country Club and the races at Chester, as well as the zoo, regatta and fairground.

John Blakeley Jnr. behind the camera for the shooting of 'Lovely Weekend'

This lacklustre little offering was the last film worked on by John E. Blakeley, as he had, under his pseudonym of Anthony Toner, written its story. Dorothy Stimson also returned to help and was as usual

126

responsible for editing. The film's only other note of interest was that it was Mancunian's only foray into colour production. Although having received its British Board of Film Classification certificate during May 1956, the film didn't gain a release until 1958. With its eventual distribution being undertaken by Rank, 'Lovely Weekend' managed a fairly widespread release.

By the mid-1950s, the Blakeley family was once again to be associated with cinema ownership. As a way of investing for his sons' future and in order to give them further income, John E. part invested in the newly formed L&B Cinemas. The 'L' being Arthur Lee, the father-in-law of John Jnr. who together along with Tom Blakeley formed the directorship of the company. L&B had cinemas in, Northenden, Monton, and Openshaw where as changing circumstances would dictate, Arthur Lee would eventually undertake most of their future operations.

Although the BBC had taken over the Dickenson Road Studio in 1954 and indeed had broadcast from there, it was not officially opened until after BBC engineers had completed alterations. This transpired in April of 1956; just one month before Granada Television opened the country's first purpose built television studios in Manchester. Granada's arrival in Manchester was to have a bearing on the future for Tom and John Blakeley and the Mancunian technicians. For the Blakeleys' were to negotiate a contract with the commercial Television Company under which the Mancunian Film Unit would work freelance for them out of the Parsonage. This unit consisted of about five men including cameramen and sound recordist. Using their own equipment they worked totally independent of Granada. Although much of the material they shot was for use in the local Granada News shows, they did also shoot many external scenes for use in a variety of programmes.

Since the sale of the studio, John E. had taken more of a back seat in the business. Having suffered ill-health for some time, he had been leaving most of the work to his two sons. Though not perhaps liking to admit the fact, he was now all but essentially retired. Not being so actively involved now, John E. was able to spend more time at home and with his grandchildren. It was now possible for him to partake in a leisurely round of golf, a sport that he had loved enormously and at which he had won many trophies. John E. was also a keen football fan and for many years had attended the games of his beloved Manchester City. Now there would be no more rushing from Saturday board meetings at the studio to Maine Road as the journey could now be taken at a more relaxed pace. He would also have more time to study the form of racehorses, for he was known to have an occasional flutter. Since the sale of the studio, he had found himself in a position to indulge in what some might refer to, as luxuries. He purchased, what was at the time, one of the most expensive cars on the market; an Armstrong Siddley Sapphire. The car was so big he was unable to garage it at his home forcing him to leave it at his son's. John E. never needed an excuse or reason to buy gifts for his family or to be amongst them and his newly acquired free time enabled him to do this more often. The family had always been the most important part of his life and Christmas time was always extra special to the Blakeley's. Many a Christmas or Boxing Day was spent together in celebration at the Grand Hotel, Manchester. These and other family occasions were exactly that, 'for family only', though John E. and his wife Bella both loved to entertain friends, and this along with theatre visits helped to occupy his time.

During the second half of 1957, much discussion had taken place regarding the future direction of The Mancunian Film Corporation. With Tom and John Jnr. now basically running the business, the pair decided that they should form a new company. This company, 'Blakeley Films (Manchester) Ltd', based at the Parsonage, was to be the new film production arm for Mancunian. Any plans that lay in the pipeline for future production however, had to be put on hold due to the sad death of John E. Blakeley Sr. on 20th February 1958. He had died at his home in Heaton Mersey, Stockport, following a two-month illness. On hearing of Blakeley's death, George Formby was reported as saying. *"He found a lot of talent. These days now all they want is a gimmick. But John didn't want gimmicks he was always looking for good solid talent. "He never produced any epics but he did a lot for British films. "John made people laugh when they needed it most"*. Norman Evans was brief but sincere when he said, *"He was a wonderful man, I owe him a lot"*.

As with every decade, the 1950s had seen varying shifts in social changes, lifestyle, trends, fashion, and music. Cinema had been feeling its own effects and was soon to go through a stage of metamorphosis, especially with the increasing popularity of television wearing away at the attendance figures. Manchester however, at the start of the 1960s, saw the Mancunian office at the Parsonage still busy and the Mancunian Film Unit was regularly occupied filming for Granada Television. While on the renting side, a new deal was arranged with Anglo Amalgamated, under which Mancunian was to distribute their films to the north-west of England. Mancunian also continued the procedure started by John E. of making 'shorts' edited from their previous films. During 1959 Jewel and Warriss appeared in a 49-minute featurette *'Stick 'em Up'* extracted from *'Let's have a Murder'*, and also in *'Sergeant's Pets'*, and *'Army Capers'* both cut from *'What-a-Carry-On!'*. The Norman Evans feature *'Over the Garden Wall'* was cut back to form a sixty-minute featurette, while a one-reeler *'Evans Above'* came from the same film. The following year, three more features went through the same process to yield four eighteen-minute shorts. As a consequence Frank Randle was back on the big screen in *'Full House'*, extracted from *'Somewhere in Politics'*, *'As You Were'* from *'It's a Grand Life'*, and *'Seaside Frolics'* and *'Tonight's the Nite'* both cut from *'Holidays with Pay'*. Naturally, no film footage was ever wasted at Mancunian and even the circus scenes filmed for *'Elephants Come to Town'* were re-used along with surplus footage to make several one-reel interest films. These included *"Visit to the Zoo'*, *'Circus Parade'*, *The Big Show'*, and *'Zoo Time'*.

On the production side, the next few years were to bring a variation in output that would see Tom Blakeley producing ten films, most of which would be Mancunian or Blakeley Films productions. The exceptions were those produced by Planet Film Productions, an enterprise that Tom Blakeley and Bill Chalmers had originally formed as a distribution company. Besides Planet, Tom during the sixties was to be a director of several other companies including, Mancunian Film Corporation, Blakeley Films (M/cr) Ltd, L&B Cinemas and Skillacts Ltd. He was also to remain as a director of Films Studios Manchester, for although it had been inactive since being sold the company was not to be officially dissolved until 1968.

So, while John Blakeley Jnr. remained more or less in charge of the Mancunian Film Unit, it is clear that the rest of the Mancunian/Blakeley production history rests with Tom Blakeley. Consequently, what follows is a somewhat condensed version of the last years of Blakeley film production. Still, no matter which official company was to actually produce the oncoming films, they were with the press or trade journals to be ever categorised as *'Mancunian'* productions.

Whether future productions were deliberately planned as 'co-features' and/or 'B' movies is uncertain, however, this was certainly the pattern that they were to follow. It was not surprising, bearing in mind his upbringing that the first film Tom put into production since the death of his father, was a comedy. Tom though, had learned the lesson of the diminishing audience for his father's preference of comedy-burlesque, and intended that this new film should follow in the same vein as his earlier *'Love's a Luxury'*. That is, light-hearted entertainment based on a stage play. Consequently, having acquired the rights to the play *'Widows are Dangerous'* by June Garland, it was adapted by Brock Williams into the filmable screenplay *'In Walked Eve'*. Although the film was to be produced by 'Blakeley's Films (Manchester.) Ltd', a financial deal was made with 'Butcher's Films Services', which effectively made it a co-production. Indeed the completed film was billed as 'Mancunian Film Corporation Ltd' presents a 'Mancunian Butcher Production'. With *'In Walked Eve'*, Tom was confident that the way forward was still with comedies and said at the time. *"They can keep their dramas. "They can have 'em. "I'll stick to comedy. I know something about that"*. It is perhaps understandable that Tom had made such a statement, for his working life had been occupied in what was a comedic environment. First hand, he had seen how his father had worked with the music hall comedians. Tom had worked alongside John E. on his films, learning all he could. Films and comedy had gone hand in glove with the Blakeley family and was in their blood. Tom had clearly inherited the feeling for this genre. As the cameras turned on *'In Walked Eve'* at Walton Studios, London, in October 1959, Tom was asked by one trade paper how he could produce a 'feature' film in such a short time. *"We all work hard, very hard.* He said. *"We settle on a script and the way we are going to do it and we don't alter it on the floor unless we absolutely have to"*. With a budget of over £20,000, the film seems likely to have been conceived as a 'co-feature'. The film's director Francis Searle explained to us the apparent differences between a 'co-feature' and a 'B' movie. *"Both would have shooting schedules of not much more than three weeks, 'B' films usually ran for between 50-minutes and 65-minutes, whereas 'co-features' obviously ran longer up to 90-minutes. 'B' films certainly cost much less than the £20,000-plus that was being spent on 'In Walked Eve', usually £12,000 to £14,000 up to the £20,000 mark. Of course the obvious difference was that a 'B' film only achieved around 15% or 20% of the marketing while a 'co-feature' shared equal billing and usually had a bigger star actor. "The biggest outlay for the producer was in hiring actors and studios. On 'In Walked Eve' the cast as I recall included Hy Hazell a delightful piece of pulchritude and Garry Marsh a reliable sort. "The shooting schedule meant it was an arduous task for everyone concerned, it was taxing but of course we were all professionals and worked well".* The story was a farcical comedy set in the quiet English village of Warlock. Here Louise Kingston (Hy Hazell) has turned her quaint cottage into the Willow Tree Tearooms. The villagers can foresee nothing but scandal however, as Louise is soon found in a compromising situation with the local inspector, Roland Axebridge (Garry Marsh). The arrival of her daughter, Eve (Sally Smith) provides an opportunity for more innocuous sexual jokes and double entendres.

Probably realising that the story wasn't strong enough to carry the film as a 'co-feature', its running time was trimmed to around 64 minutes making it suitable for a supporting film and was submitted to the British Board of Film Classification during November 1959. However, although *"In Walked Eve'* was trade shown in March of 1960, it encountered trouble in obtaining a release. Consequently, during September the film underwent a name change to *"Trouble with Eve"*, even so it wasn't until May of 1961 that it eventually managed to gain a circuit release. These problems could have been one reason why Tom decided to try a different type of picture.

BUTCHER'S FILM DISTRIBUTORS LTD.
present
ROBERT URQUHART
HY HAZELL
GARRY MARSH
trouble
VERA DAY
SALLY SMITH
WITH
eve
Directed by FRANCIS SEARLE
Produced by TOM BLAKELEY
A MANCUNIAN - BUTCHER PRODUCTION

(Left) 'Trouble with Eve' eventually gained a circuit release as a second feature. The film was also released in America under the title of 'In Trouble with Eve'.

John E. Blakeley's one axiom had been to make films cheaply. Tom was now evidently aware that the only way to carry on his father's credo was not to compete in the main feature film market but instead to concentrate on the demand for supporting pictures. Times and tastes had moved on. There was still a healthy market for comedies as was being somewhat ironically confirmed by the success of the early *'Carry On'* films, which if nothing else proved John E. Blakeley was a man before his time. The past few years had though also seen the emergence of 'free thinking' teenagers, bringing to the fore their non-conformity, so-called lack of sexual virtues and of course their Rock 'n' Roll music. Teenagers were now making up a large part of cinema audiences and they had money to spend. Their issues were also to prove a commodity in the content of films, even if only treated as a passing fad by most producers.

In the time, it eventually took *'Trouble with Eve'* to realise a release, Tom had completed his next production *'Rag Doll'*, given it a trade showing and gained it a circuit release. This latest production was very different from anything normally associated with the Blakeley name. For this, and his next production, were to be 'youth' orientated. Screenwriters' Brock Williams and Derry Quinn had completed a story centring on the problems of a seventeen-year-old girl. The star of *'Rag Doll'* was Jess Conrad, a young, up and coming actor cum singer. Jess had already had one small screen credit with a role in *'Serious Charge'* in which Cliff Richard also appeared. Starting out as an actor Conrad had made a name for himself as Barney, a Rock 'n' Roll singer in a television play *'Rock-a-bye Barney'*. Not long after, Jack Good the mastermind behind television pop shows *'65 Special'* and *'Oh Boy!'* put Conrad in another hit music show *'Wham!'*. Jess Conrad recalled, *"I think 'Rag Doll' was sort of written for and around me. I'd just been in 'Wham' and Tom Blakeley had gone to see my agent. They both knew that it would be important for me to be in a film especially at that time when all the teenagers were going to the cinema"*. Set in London's Soho, *'Rag Doll'* is a highly moralistic crime drama. Jess Conrad plays Joe Shane, a would-be singer who falls in love with teenage runaway Carol, played by model Christina Gregg. When Carol falls pregnant, they decide to start a new life abroad. Nevertheless, to do so needs money. Joe breaks in to the home of Mort Wilson, Carol's café owner boss played by Kenneth Griffith. In a bungled attempt at robbery, Joe fatally shoots Mort and is himself wounded. Running from the law with Carol in tow he is eventually tracked down and dies in the arms of his lover. Although Lance Comfort was the film's director, Jack

132

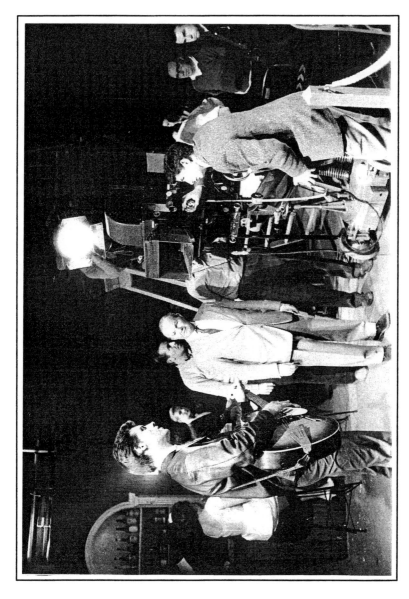

Jess Conrad (left) with Director Lance Comfort (centre) on the Walton Studios set of 'Rag Doll'

Good directed the musical scenes. Good was reputed to have earned a substantial fee for his work on *'Rag Doll'*. One scene however, which included Conrad singing the title song, was eventually cut from the film. Another song though, *'Why Am I Living,'* which was included in the picture, was eventually released by Decca Records on the 'B' side to *'This Pullover'*. *'Rag Doll'* was shot at the studios at Walton in November of 1960. The small town of Walton-on-Thames is where Conrad finished his schooling. *"I was a big movie fan when I left school"*, recalled Jess. *"It was an incredible feeling to go back to Walton and work in the studio. "Tom Blakeley produced it on a tight budget but he looked after us very well. "The three or four week shoot was altogether a very happy experience"*.

As a supporting feature, *'Rag Doll'* like *'Trouble with Eve'* gained a release on the ABC cinema circuit. *'Rag Doll'* went out with the Bob Monkhouse starring vehicle *'Weekend with Lulu'*, while *'Trouble with Eve'* supported the Anglo-Amalgamated feature *'Payroll'*.

For his next production, Tom Blakeley hired studio space at Shepperton. Here during August of 1961, under the direction of Lance Comfort, *'Painted Smile'* another dose of youth orientated crime drama was shot in just three weeks. Lance Comfort had worked in the film industry since the mid-1920s, working initially on medical films as an animator and cameraman. Moving into the commercial market, he worked for some time with producer John Baxter and eventually directed his first film in 1941. During the 1940s he was to direct several top box-office attractions ranging from the wartime espionage of *'Escape to Danger'* to the slapstick of *'Old Mother Riley, Detective'*. It was however, with his first-rate direction on melodramatic features like *'Hatter's Castle'* and *'Bedelia'* that he excelled. When this style of film went out of vogue, especially when the late 1950s brought in the so-called 'new wave' of directors, (the likes of John Schlesinger and Lindsay Anderson), Comfort had to settle for less prestigious work of a 'B' movie and television director. It was no doubt the talent of Comfort, which managed to lift the Blakeley productions, if not to the heights of 'cult' status, then certainly above the welter of 'B' movie dross that was coming out of British studios at this time.

As an added attraction for the teenage audience, the cast of *'Painted Smile'* also included the popular singer of the time, Craig Douglas. It is interesting to note that Blakeley, in offering the small role of nightclub singer to Douglas, had already turned down the Beatles. While casting for the film, the Beatles, through Brian Epstein, came forward.

Tom unfortunately rejected them as he thought they were too young. Recalling this event a few years later, at a time when the Beatles were at the height of their fame, he said, *"I asked; who are the Beatles? "Quite honestly, I didn't think they were ready for it. "I was proved wrong. But I'm not sore about it"*. The cast of *'Painted Smile'* included Liz Fraser, Kenneth Griffith, Peter Reynolds and Tony Wickert. The story revolves around student Tom (Wickert) who, celebrating a £100 windfall with two companions, attends a sleazy club. In a drunken stupor, he is conned by Jo (Fraser), who escorts him back to her flat. Here her partner, Mark (Reynolds) as the 'outraged husband' is

Liz Fraser and Kenneth Griffith in 'The Painted Smile'.

supposedly to confront Tom. Unfortunately, the local Soho gangster, (Griffith) arrives first and murders Mark. When the young couple arrive and discover the body, Tom unthinking touches the knife, Jo explains that the police will probably blame him. Consequently, she persuades him to dispose of the body. She then disappears, leaving as expected the

135

police to search for Tom as the main suspect. His only way of clearing himself is in finding Jo. Obviously, with much of the work on his films being carried out in London studios, it was inevitable that he should also have offices there. Though, as with his father before him, Tom remained close to his northern roots. He continued to live in Wilmslow, Manchester, and much of the planning for the films was carried out from his small office at the Parsonage in Manchester. Actors, William Lucas and Kenneth Cope, who were to appear respectively in the next two Blakeley films, the *The Break'* and *'Tomorrow at Ten'*, and together in the later *'Night of the Big Heat'*, both have vivid memories of Tom Blakeley and of his northern friendliness. Perhaps, being Manchester born, Bill Lucas may have felt a close affinity to Blakeley. Certainly, he was well aware of his father and of the old Manchester Studio. *"I actually worked in that studio"*, Bill told us. *"It was during the 1960s, when the BBC had taken over, and I did a play from there. "It was actually a very pleasant feeling knowing that one was in the building where that wonderful comic Frank Randle had made his films - magic he was!"* Speaking of Tom, Bill Lucas continued, *"Tom was an extremely nice guy. He had no pretensions or anything like that, he was very happy making the films he did. "He remained rooted in Manchester and I remember calling at his house on Wilmslow Road. Michael, his son, had a habit of occupying the whole terrace while taking cars to pieces and putting them back together again. It wasn't surprising really that he should have gone into the technical side of the business. "One thing that has stuck with me about Tom, was the way he looked after everyone on the set, small things but appreciated. He was such a nice guy to work for."* Kenneth Cope echoed similar sentiments when he told us; *"I remember him being so kind and pleasant. During the shooting of 'Tomorrow at Ten' he'd come on the set and was always looking after our welfare. With a lot of producers you could almost get ill-treatment but I think because Tom was from the north he looked after us better. I'm not talking about fees or financial matters, I mean with cups of tea - the little things. There was a general northern concern for ones well-being. "John Gregson and Robert Shaw were the stars, but Tom was still very, very nice to me, lowly Kenneth. I've never forgotten him".*

What is significant about *'The Break'* and *'Tomorrow at Ten'* is that both films were a step up from the 'supporting' feature bracket. Though not quite strong enough to pull in the audiences on their own, they were coupled with other films as 'co-features' or 'Double-bills' and did extremely good business on the major circuits. Both carried the copyright line of the Mancunian Film Corporation and again were to be directed by Lance Comfort. The first went into production at

Shepperton Studios in January 1962, while *'Tomorrow at Ten'* was shot at the MGM Borehamwood Studios in June of the same year. Initially, it went into production as *'The Golliwog'*, but as the title, in today's terminology would have been seen as racist or offensive, was altered to *'Chance to Live'* before finally, at the suggestion of film editor John Trumper, becoming *'Tomorrow at Ten'*.

Headed by a strong cast, *'The Break'* starred William Lucas, Tony Britton, Robert Urquhart and Eddie Byrne. The story told the tale of an escaped convict, who while on the run, kills a private detective that he mistakenly believes to be on his trail. The complex plot also involves smugglers and a second murder before the villain meets his own end. Filmed from the convict's viewpoint, *'The Break'* contrasted with *'Tomorrow at Ten'*, which followed events from the perspective of the authorities. Acknowledged by many as perhaps being Tom Blakeley's best offering from this period – thanks in no uncertain terms to the directorial skill of Lance Comfort - *'Tomorrow at Ten'* contains a good storyline that still holds up well today. The film, a thriller, tells of a race against time to find a kidnapped boy imprisoned with a time bomb, after his abductor has died without revealing the child's whereabouts. John Gregson, Robert Shaw and Alex Clunes gave good performances. Again, a good strong cast had been assembled; Gregson was still a top box office name having appeared in many memorable British films including *'Genevieve'*, *'Angels One Five'* and *'The Battle of the River Plate'*. Robert Shaw had been a character actor in films since the early 1950s but at this time was well known from the television series *'The Buccaneers'*. Shaw was of course to become a big international star with such films as *'The Sting'*, *'Jaws'* and *'The Deep'*. Gregson played Inspector

Tony BRITTON
William LUCAS
Eddie BYRNE
Robert URQUHART

THE BREAK

Newspaper style advertising for 'The Break'

137

Starring John Gregson and Robert Shaw, 'Tomorrow at Ten' was undoubtedly the best of the 1960s Tom Blakeley Productions.

Parnell with Kenneth Cope as his assistant Sergeant Grey. KennethCope recalled *"I think perhaps Tom Blakeley had a bit of idolisation for people like Johnnie (Gregson) who was of course a big star then, but that didn't change his attitude towards us lesser mortals. "We had a lot of fun on that film. "We'd been using this old police car, a Wolsey or Riley, and we were going back to the studio along the North Circular Road, when we decided to have a bit of fun. "Driving in front of us were two young girls in an open sports car and Johnnie said 'lets pull them over'. "So we sounded the police bell and the young women pulled over. We got out of the car and walked over to them, Johnnie wearing his trench coat and me with my somewhat lesser looking raincoat we rather cruelly hinted that we were real coppers. "Naughty really but just a bit of fun. "John Gregson was such a nice man as too was, as I say Tom Blakeley".*

With the production of 'Room at the Top', the early sixties were to see the emergence in British cinema of what was to be termed 'new wave'. New directors brought to the screen social protest illustrated by the young working-class males, the so-called 'angry young men'. Films like 'Saturday Night and Sunday Morning' (60), 'A Taste of Honey' (61), 'A Kind of Loving' (62), and 'The Loneliness of the Long Distance Runner' (62), were all typical of this new genre. Most used genuine northern towns to depict working-class life as it really was lived. Tom Blakeley having a northern film-producing pedigree was himself, during 1962, bemoaning the fact that he couldn't find a suitable script with which he could emulate the success of these northern-based working-class films. Not since 'It's a Grand Life', had a Blakeley film had a north of England feel. Perhaps with some justification he felt confident that he could produce a northern drama or comedy. Speaking at the time, he said, *"...we just can't find a decent script. "There's no shortage of scripts – we get a least two dozen a week submitted to read – but there's a desperate shortage of good ones. "...It would be nice to find a North Country subject to use".*

Before any more productions were to get underway though, changes were taking place at the Parsonage, in Manchester. It was now decided that the Mancunian office would close, and that all the usual business that had been carried out from there would be transferred to the Blakeley owned 'Prince's Cinema' at Eccles.

Although the films produced by Tom had been done so through either of the two Blakeley family run Companies (Blakeley Films or The Mancunian Film Corporation), it was however, through Planet Film Distributors that they had their distribution. Whereas, Mancunian had, during the time of John E. Blakeley been able to distribute its own films in the northern territories, Tom obviously realised that a wider distribution was now needed and consequently 'Planet' was formed. Besides the marketing of his own product Tom and partner Bill Chalmers - who had joined Tom after leaving Butcher's Film Services - also distributed films from other producers including the Helion Production '*Touch of Death*' and the Avon production *Journey into Nowhere*'. During 1963, Blakeley and Chalmers decided to move Planet into the production side of the business. Consequently, there was now only to be one more Blakeley Films/Mancunian production, this being the melodramatic thriller '*Blind Corner*'. Shot at Pinewood during October 1963, the film again tried to capitalise on the pop music market by basing the story around a songwriter. William Sylvester starred as Paul Gregory a blind composer who is deeply in love with his wife Anne, played by Barbara Shelley. Anne takes great pleasure in living the life of luxury that Paul's pop compositions bring and encourages him to write more, much to the detriment of his real desire to finish his elaborate concerto. Anne also happens to be cheating on Paul by carrying on an affair with Rickie Seldon (Alex Davion), an artist who is infatuated by her. So much so that Anne persuades Rickie that he should kill Paul so the pair can claim his money and disappear together. Paul's secretary Joan Marshall (Elizabeth Shepherd) not only longs for him to complete his concerto, but also is fully aware of Anne's infidelity, she herself also secretly loves Paul. Anne is also deceiving Rickie however, as she is really in love with Mike

'Blind Corner' had an American release with the title 'Man in the Dark'

140

Williams (Mark Eden), Paul's manager and so-called friend. The couple are merely using Rickie, and plan for him to be caught by the authorities after he has murdered Paul. Paul eventually works out what is happening and despite being blind, puts his other highly acute senses to work and in the total darkness of his apartment, a dangerous life or death scenario is played out. With 'good' being triumphant the film ends with Paul and his secretary Joan going off together. With this film, Lance Comfort was back working in the field of melodrama and again brought to the production much worth, with enough twists and turns to satisfy most movie fans. Once more a popular singer of the day, Ronnie Carroll was given a small role and a number of songs to sing. With a running time of 80-minutes, the film secured a 'co-feature' billing.

The year 1963 had seen the first production from Planet. Now producing totally independent from family ties, Tom was firstly to make a short 63-minute second feature, *The Marked One*' directed by Francis Searle and starring William Lucas, before turning his sights to bigger things. The next film, *Devil's of Darkness*' was to be a 'first' on several accounts. As a gothic horror, it was certainly new ground for Tom Blakeley. It was also the first time any film associated with the Blakeley name had been shot in colour (excluding the short *Lovely Weekend*'), and their first 'X' certificate. Being produced as a main or 'first' feature obviously had increased its expenditure and at £110,000 was certainly Tom's costliest to date. Directed by Lance Comfort – who was making his first and only foray into this genre – and starring William Sylvester, the film was shot at the Pinewood Studios.

Joining with the popular Hammer horror cycle of films, *Devils of Darkness*' was well received by audiences as Tom Blakeley pointed out at the time of its release. *"It's our costliest film but it seems to be going well at the box office...a cinema in Norwich put on a special midnight matinee because so many people wanted to see it"*.

With the next two productions, *Island of Terror*' and *The Night of the Big Heat*', Tom kept the shocks and chills coming, albeit now from a sci-fi perspective. Both films again were shot at Pinewood with direction undertaken by Terence Fisher. Fisher was well-known to fans of the horror / sci-fi genre having worked with Hammer since the early 1950s and having directed many of their successes including *The Curse of Frankenstein*', *The Gorgon*', *The Two Faces of Dr. Jekyll*', *The Mummy*' and countless others. Two stars from Hammer's stable of actors were

141

brought in with both Peter Cushing and Christopher Lee appearing in *'Island of Terror'*. Lee also appeared, alongside Patrick Allen and William Lucas, in *'The Night of the Big Heat'*. Perhaps not up to the standards of Hammer Productions, these films were still nonetheless well received at the box-office. Indeed as it turned out, *'Island of Terror'* was to prove to be Tom Blakeley's most successful film.

Between making the two sci-fi films Blakeley had been outlining his future plans and in a well-publicised statement, reported that he had acquired the rights to the novel *'The Long Run South'* by Alan Williams, with which he hoped to enter the 'big time'. Tom also added that he hoped to begin shooting in Spain during May [1966] with Burt Lancaster perhaps taking the lead. Mike Blakeley recalled that his father was indeed looking at Burt Lancaster and also Richard Chamberlain – popular at the time through his *'Dr. Kildare'* television shows - but apparently, the actor whom he most favoured was Curt Jurgens. Sadly, after almost two years of negotiations and planning, Tom was eventually forced to abandon the 'big budgeted' project at the final hurdle, when he fell just £10,000 short of the £500,000 needed.

Although Tom Blakeley was only in his early fifties, the constant travelling between Manchester and London, and the two-year stress of trying to get *'The Long Run South'* in production was beginning to take its toll. The pressure and the strain had all added to his health problems and he was now suffering with Angina attacks. What he really needed was rest and relaxation. Consequently, Tom Blakeley slipped into retirement leaving *'The Night of the Big Heat'* as his final contribution to the British Cinema. Planet, the distribution company, continued only for a few more years with Bill Chalmers continuing to run it, as a hobby more than anything.

Now basically in retirement Tom was spending most of his time at his Manchester home, though he did remain as managing Director of the Mancunian Film Corporation. Though Mancunian, from their base at the Prince's Cinema was still renting out their old films, the main activity was centred on the Mancunian Film Unit. As the Prince's Cinema was still functioning as a cinema, the Unit had to use an area under the stage as their base. Tom Blakeley's son, Mike, joined the Unit in 1965 as an assistant on sound and camera and he recalled. *"When I started we needed a film crew of five people as we were using a big hefty movie camera from the States, a twelve-volt car battery, a converter, sound equipment, as well as the supplementary stuff like mikes and film stock. Imagine,*

142

five men, every bit of equipment all together cramped under the stage waiting for a call out from Granada, not what you'd call ideal conditions". By 1971, Mike had gained enough experience to be promoted to cameraman. A year later and he personally introduced a revolution in television newsgathering by setting up two man news crews. This he achieved by importing more easily manoeuvrable and up-to-date camera equipment from America, and by 1973 had four two-man crews contracted out to Granada. Mike himself, was now also gaining a reputation for his work and over three consecutive years he was nominated for a BAFTA Award as Cameraman of the year. The film crews, although mainly shooting news items for Granada were often also called upon to film various location scenes for a wide range of other programmes. Their work could have been seen on anything from the local documentaries to *'World in Action'* and even top soap opera *'Coronation Street'*. On one occasion John Blakeley Jnr. was filming a news piece on the stage of the Manchester Opera House featuring the D'Oyly Carte Opera Company. Unfortunately, John's camera work was apparently marred by the inadequacies of his soundman. In due time the person concerned was to turn his back on sound and concentrate instead on camera work. Working on many occasions with John Blakeley he obviously learned a great deal and this 'sound man' who wasn't a 'good sound man' was eventually to become Granada's star cameraman George Jessie Turner. George went on to win several awards as the *'World in Action'* chief cameraman.

L&B Cinemas, having already closed two of their venues was finally wound up as a company in 1976 after the Prince's Cinema had ceased trading the previous year. As a result, the Mancunian Film Unit was no longer confined to the cramped space beneath the stage. Though eventually, through a matter of convenience, they moved across to the Granada building, initially working from out of their reception area before acquiring a room of their own.

In 1979, the Mancunian film unit effectively ceased to be, when all the film crews were taken over by Granada Television. For the next two years, the old Prince's Cinema remained as the distribution for the Mancunian Film Corporation's products. By 1981, with a dwindling market that was mainly limited to Children's matinees and one day only Sunday showings, the company was finally wound-up in July. It was estimated that after paying off debts that there would be a surplus of £17,472.

The legacy left behind by Mancunian is far greater than any amount of money. The Blakeley family were certainly unique to the northern film business and Manchester can be proud of John E. Blakeley, a man who worked tirelessly throughout his life. Blakeley stood head and shoulders above the countless other 'minnows' of the film world that collectively were the very backbone of the British Film Industry. The Blakeley story has of course not yet ended, as today the Blakeley family continues to work in the media of film and television thus keeping alive the tradition started back in 1908 by James Blakeley. Mike Blakeley now heads Blakeley Films and since 1997, on leaving Granada Television has travelled the world as a freelance Director and Lighting Cameraman. Both of his children have now also entered the business with father and son recently having worked together on a feature, while Mike's daughter has worked with the BBC team that brought 'Children's Hospital' to the screen. In his work, firstly for Granada TV and latterly as a freelance, Mike has worked on many award-winning programmes and has also been the recipient of personal awards. John E. Blakeley would have been proud.

Appendix 1
Betty Driver & 'Boots! Boots!'

During the writing of this book, we have fortunately been able to view many of the films made by John E. Blakeley. The George Formby film *'Boots! Boots!'* was originally released as an eighty minute film but for years this version had been lost, leaving only a fifty-two minute edited re-release version. However, during 2000 James Mockoski an American student, undertaking a thesis on Bert Tracey at the University of Norwich came across an almost complete version.

Of course when we began our own initial writings about *'Boots! Boots!'* we were doing so by scrutinising the then only film available, the fifty-two minute copy. In this version, Betty Driver – of *'Coronation Street'* fame – was credited on the titles but did not appear in the film. We originally contacted the actress to ask if she recalled the film. The following is taken from our original draft.

Another inconvenience was the fact that the filming was taking place during a very cold October in 1933 and with very little heating in the room, the task had become a considerably arduous one. Betty Driver known to millions of people from her years in the television soap opera *'Coronation Street'* told us; *"It was indeed difficult and very cold during the filming - still as they say, that's show business"*. As a twelve-year-old child, Betty had been appearing with a repertory company in Longsight, Manchester. Blakeley, George Formby and his wife Beryl all saw the young Miss Driver perform and afterwards went to offer her a part in the closing cabaret scene of the film. In the company of her mother, an excited Betty arrived at the studio on the first day of rehearsals. Giving her all, she soon had the watching technicians enthralled with her talent, all of whom, after she had finished her number showed their appreciation with loud cheers and applause. Apparently witnessing this whole scene from the corner of the room had been a stony-faced Beryl. Betty recalls; *"With jealousy in her eyes she turned and said 'if that kid sings - I'm off'"*. Of course, with Formby being his star, Blakeley had no option other than to let Betty go. *"John E. Blakeley was very nice to me"*, added Betty, *"and he kept my name on the credits which was good"*.

145

However, with the discovery of the more complete version of *'Boots!*
Boots!' it can be seen that Betty Driver's song was not in point of fact
cut. Her appearance in the closing cabaret scene, where she is seen
singing with Harry Hudson's band, is actually included.

James Mockoski, during research for his thesis on Bert Tracey came
into contact with film collector David Wyatt. It was discovered that
David had a nitrate version of *'Boots! Boots!'*. It wasn't until James
viewed it that they realised it-contained scenes not included in the re-
release version. Today, now having viewed the newly found film Betty
Driver has acknowledged that she was indeed in the final version of
'Boots! Boots!'. She told us, *"Fancy John Blakeley leaving my scene in, I can't
believe it as I didn't think it was very good, but still at 12 what do you expect".*
Happily, plans are now underway to bring together elements from
both versions to make available an almost complete rendering of the
film.

Appendix 2

A George Formby sketch
from Boots! Boots!

The scene opens in a hairdressing salon/cum barbershop. Formby's character John Willie is idling his time away sitting in the barbers' chair while strumming his uke. While mumbling to himself about working morning, noon and night a lady enters.

Lady: *"Good morning"*
John Willie: *"Oh good morning madam"* (Stands up and gets out of chair)
Lady: *"Are you the hairdresser"*
John Willie: *"well no not exactly. But I work when the fella's having his day off you see. Take seat will you missus"*
Lady: *"You can attend to me"*
John Willie: *"Oh I can attend to you all right".* (John Willie drapes towel over lady) *"Nice weather we're having isn't it"*
Lady: *"Oh yes, very"*
John Willie: *"There's a lot of nice weather to come an' all"*
Lady: *"Is there?"*
John Willie: *"Yes, all next week's not been touched yet"*
(Having taken the lady's handbag for safekeeping John Willie starts to rummage through it)
John Willie: *"Nice bit of stuff this"*
Lady: *"What do you mean? Put that down, that belongs to me"*
John Willie: *"Sorry, Sorry I always had taking ways though – Now what can I do for you"*
Lady: *"Well first of all I want a haircut"*
John Willie: (Feeling the lady's hair) *"Er, which one"*
Lady: *"Why all of them you fool"*
John Willie: *I well, I only wanted to be sure you see"*
Lady: *"Tell me young man have you been cutting hair long"?*
John Willie: *"No. Short as a rule"*
(John Willie walks around back of chair to the sink and picks up shaving brush and mug)
John Willie: *"Did you read the interesting news in the paper this morning"?*
Lady: *"No. Not particularly"*
John Willie: *"Snuff's gone up a ha'penny a ton"*

Lady: *"Snuff"?*
John Willie begins to lather lady's chin
John Willie: *"It's marvellous how these things happen isn't it"*
The lady, with soap in her mouth splutters as the hotel pageboy enters.
Page: (to John Willie) *"Hey Goofy, you're wanted in the Blue Room there's something wrong with the light"*
John Willie: *"In the Blue Room"?*
Page: *"Yes"*
John Willie: *"Oh I see"*
(As John Willie continues to lather the lady's chin she now begins to complain)
Lady: *"What are you doing"?*
John Willie: *"Shut up. Shut up when everybody is talking"!*
Lady: *"What on earth have you done"?*
John Willie: (to Page) *"Did you say I was wanted in the Blue Room"*
Page: *"Yes"*
John Willie: (to Page) *"Let's have a look at that paper"*
(John Willie takes newspaper from Page and sits down on the footrest of the barbers' chair)
John Willie: *"Shift your feet missus"*
(The lady splutters as she continues to wipe shaving soap from her face)
Lady: *"Shift my feet"?*
John Willie: (to lady) *"Be quiet while I'm reading will you".* (to Page) *"Well I'll go to our house. You know that horse I backed yesterday – it's come up. What price is it"?*
Page: *"13 to 4 on"*
John Willie: *"13 to 4 on, let me see that's er.. thruppence each way, 13 to 4 on that brings in fourpence-ha'penny doesn't it. Fourpence-ha'penny and three-ha'pence is sixpence. I er.. say missus..."*
Lady: (who throughout all this has continued to rid herself of the offending soap) *"Well"*
John Willie: *"I suppose I'll be getting a tip for this when I've finished won't I"?*
Lady: *"Just depends how you do your work"*
John Willie: *"Well I think I'd better have my tip now and be on the safe side hadn't I"*
Lady: (Hands him a tip) *"Well you saucy monkey you"*
John Willie: (to lady) *"Yes - Thank you very much".* (to Page) *"Now that's fourpence-ha'penny and sixpence and fourpence-ha'pence to come is a shilling, go and put me a shilling on 'Fanlight Fanny'.*
Page: *What, both ways"?*

148

John Willie: *"Yes then I'll be sure of it coming back"*
Page: *"Well don't forget the light"*
John Willie: Go on. *I know – don't start bossing me"*
Lady: *"Now look here young man I came her to have a haircut and waves not to have my face plastered all over with that rubbish"*
John Willie: *"Yes. I'm awfully sorry I was carried away for the minute"*
Lady: *"Carried away"?*
John Willie: *"I won't do it again"*
Lady: *"I hope you won't"*
John Willie: *"You want your hair cutting don't you"?*
Lady: *"I want my hair cutting"*
(John Willie starts to remove hairpins from lady's hair)
John Willie: *"What do you mess your hair up with all these things for"*
Lady: *"Oh I'll take them out if you're in a hurry"*
John Willie: *"You never see a man going about with things like that in his hair"*
Lady: *"Well men are men I've found that to be"*
(With hairpins removed John Willie starts to run his fingers through the hair)
John Willie: *"Now let me see now - a haircut – you did say this was hair didn't you"?*
Lady: *"What do you mean? Of course I said it was hair"*
(After picking up a pair of scissors John Willie decides they are too small and exchanges them for a large pair of shears. Singing a song to himself he lowers the barbers' chair flat and proceeds to cut large lumps off of the lady's hair)
Lady: *"You're pulling my hair"*
John Willie: *"Oh that's all right you won't have any to pull in a minute. I'm cutting it beautiful for you"* (Climbing all over the prostrate lady he continues to lop off clumps of hair) *"you're all right"*
Lady: *"I'm not all right"*
John Willie: *"Be still, don't worry yourself or else I'll throw you out altogether"*
Lady: *"You'll what? Oh you villain of a man. Well I've never been through such punishment in my life – never"*
John Willie: *"I think you'll do now – you'll be able to get up yourself now won't you"?*
Lady: *"Oh yes"*
John Willie: *"I've got to go to fix the light"*
Lady: *"I see"*
The scene ends – However several minutes later John Willie is accosted in the hotel's hallway by the irate lady screaming, *"Look what you did to me"* and chases him out of shot.

149

Wanted a Housekeeper.
A sketch from 'Somewhere in Camp'
With Frank Randle as Sebastian and Harry Korris as Gloria.

The scene opens in the living room of Sebastian where his maid is tidying a table full of letters.

Sebastian: *"Hey don't mess about with those letters they're important"*

Maid: *"I wouldn't touch them with a pole. I know what they are. They're answers to your advertisement"*

Sebastian: *"Oh, so you've read my advert 'av you"*

Maid: *"Read it! Why everybody's talking about it. I've got it off by heart. Uh – 'Wanted a Housekeeper with view to matrimony must be young and vivacious. Widow not objected to apply box 13'"*

Sebastian: *"Yes! Aye!"*

Maid: *"You ought to be ashamed of yourself"*

Sebastian: *"Now keep a civil tongue in your head will you"*

Maid: *"Just if I cared. I'm glad I gave my notice to leave on Saturday"*

Sebastian: *"O-Aye"*

Maid: *"You advertising for a wife at your time of life"*

Sebastian: *"Well why not"*

Maid: *"Why not! You old Blue Beard, you've had four wives already"*

Sebastian: *"Aye! Aye! I have that; eh...if the Lord keeps providing 'em I'll keep burying 'em* (Laughs)

(The doorbell rings)

Sebastian: *"That'll be 'er, that's the one I picked, she's young and experienced. Don't just stand there like a dying duck... Let 'er in.*

Maid: *"Why you old...* (Exits through door)

Sebastian: (Talking to himself) *"She sez she's a lovely figure. Eh, that's what I'm after"* (Becoming excited Sebastian begins to rubs his hands together in giddy expectation)

Gloria (enters room looks around with an air of disapproval). *"What a dump".* (Catching sight of Sebastian) *"Why if it isn't Old Moore"*

Sebastian: *"Good afternoon"*

Gloria: *"How do you do?"*

Sebastian: *"What a boiling piece"* – (kisses Gloria's hand) – *"Ee-Ee will you have a pinch of snuff"? – "May I offer you a seat, park it there?"*

Gloria: (Sits in chair at table opposite Sebastian) *"It's really too good of you".*

Sebastian: (Squeezes Gloria's knee) *"Ee-Ee by gum I bet you're a hot 'un".*

Gloria: *"I'm afraid I don't understand what you mean"*

Sebastian: *"In your letter you said you were young and vivacious"*
Gloria: *"Well am I not?"*
Sebastian: *"I'd like to see your vivacity"*
Gloria: *"I dare say you would but not here"*
Sebastian: *"Why not?"*
Gloria: *"Well I've come here for an interview not an operation"*
Sebastian: *"Ee-Ee I like a woman with a bit of spirit"*
Gloria: *"How old are you?"*
Sebastian: *"That's nowt to do wi'it"*. (Holds Gloria's arm) *"A man's as old as he feels"*
Gloria: *"Well you're feeling pretty well"*
Sebastian: *"I like you"*
Gloria: *"Do you?"*
Sebastian: *"Could I offer you a drop of wine?"*
Gloria: *"No, no!"* *"So you'd tempt the fair maiden with strong drink – Well just a small one"*
Sebastian: *"That's all you're getting' I'm saving this for the wedding"*.
Gloria: *"The wedding! Whose wedding?"*
Sebastian: *"Ours Glori'"*
Gloria: *"Oh! Sebastian"*
Sebastian: (pours out the last of the wine for himself) *"Here's to your bright eyes – I'm sorry there's not enough for thee love"* (gulps down the wine)
Gloria: *"Oh I wasn't particular I noticed there was a dead fly in it"*
Sebastian: (Grimaces and finally belches) *"B...rurp. Oh excuse me"*. (Rubbing hands with glee) *Ee-Ee now to business"*. (Tries to grab Gloria's knee) *"I want to get to the point at once"*
Gloria: *"I imagine that – but I haven't said yes Sebastian."*
Sebastian: *"No but you will. You're just like all the women dilly dallying about"*
Gloria: *"You're a real cave-man I can see that"*
Sebastian: *"I am an' all. Now listen Glori' I always like my honeymoons at home"*
Gloria: *"Ooh then you've been married before"?*
Sebastian: *"Oh yes four times"*
Gloria: *"Four times – then you're a foursome"*
Sebastian: *"Aye! They're all bunkered across the way in the old church yard there"*. *"Have you been married"?*
Gloria: *"Five times"*
Sebastian: *"Oh well you'll know all about it"*
Gloria: *"Mmmm"*
Sebastian: *"Have you any children"*

Gloria: *"No I never could bear children"*
Sebastian: *"What! Oh that's no good to me"*. (Rubs hands in glee) *"Eee give us a kiss"*
Gloria: *"No"*
Sebastian: *"Go on"*
Gloria: *"No, No, I shall thrash you"*
(Gloria moves away from Sebastian and relocates to the settee, where sitting crossed legged she provocatively shows her garter. Sebastian follows giving Randle's usual lecherous laugh, rubbing his hands he begins to strut chicken-like. He drops his handkerchief at Gloria's feet and bends down to retrieve it. Whereupon Gloria suspecting that he is trying to see something he shouldn't swings her leg and hits Sebastian across the face)
Gloria: *"Oh a thousand pardons, I'm sure you'll excuse a poor weak woman"*
Sebastian: *"Weak woman! You'd have kicked my teeth out if I'd had any in"*
Gloria: *"Won't you sit beside me"*?
Sebastian: *"Aye! Now you're talking"*. *"Did I tell you that story"*?
Gloria: *"Story"* -*"I don't want to hear it"* – *"What's it about"*?
Sebastian: *"It's about a honeymoon couple"*
(Sebastian laughs and pushes Gloria's leg whereby he notices her garter)
Sebastian: *"Oh I beg your pardon. Oh elastic eh"* (continues his story) *"and on the first night"* (Gloria slaps his face) *"Ow! What's that for"*? .... *"I've forgotten the story now"*
Gloria: *"It doesn't matter I've heard it dozens of times before"*
Sebastian: *"Oh have you. "What do you think of me Gloria"*?
Gloria: *"I think you're a dirty old man"*!
Sebastian: *"What"*
Gloria: *"I said I think you're a flirty old man"*
Sebastian: *"Well it's you. You've got me. I can't help myself. Ee by eck I've had four wives an' I could go nap wi' thee Glori'. Give me a kiss"*
Gloria: *"No. No"*
Sebastian: *"Oh yes go on"*
Gloria: *"No. No"*
(Sebastian jumps up and starts his chicken-like strutting) *"Eee I'm as wick as a weasel"* (jumps onto settee and sits on backrest) *"Will you marry me"*?
Gloria: *"No"*
Sebastian: *"Oh yes"*
Gloria: *"No"*
Sebastian: *"Oh go on"*
(Settee rocks and tips over with Gloria and Sebastian falling to the floor)
Gloria: *"I've fallen for you"*
Sebastian: *"I'll get thee for this"*

152

2:3

The Human Dummy
A sketch from 'Demobbed'

The scene opens in the foyer of a hotel. Dan Young dressed as a 'toff'
in top hat and cape enters and approaches Betty Jumel.

Dan Young: *"Good Evening"*
Betty Jumel: *"Good Evening"*
Dan Young: *"Have you a view with a room"*
Betty Jumel: *"No but I've got a room with a view"*
Dan Young: *"Well that'll do, that'll do"*
Betty Jumel: *"But what kind of a view"*
Dan Young: *"Well I should say a view like you"*
Betty Jumel: *"Now enough of that or I shall call the manager"*
Dan Young: *"You can call the manager what you like, you see I'm what they
term financially embarrassed"*
Betty Jumel: *"Oh dear"*
Dan Young: *"Or in basic English I'm nearly skint"*
Betty Jumel: *"Well our charge here you know is £1 for bed and breakfast"*
Dan Young: (sharp intake of breath) *"Lot of money, lot of money. Don't you
reduce the terms for theatricals"?*
Betty Jumel: *"Well as a matter of fact we do"*
Dan Young: *"Yes. Thanks – you see I'm what they call a ventriloquist"*
Betty Jumel: *"Oh are you"*
Dan Young: *"Ahumm – I've left my dummy outside"*
Betty Jumel: *"Well now listen to me, I'm a good sport bring your dummy in
here and show me what you can do and I'll charge you...let me see...only fifteen
shillings"*
Dan Young: (sharp intake of breathe) *"In English money for the two of
us"?*
Betty Jumel: *"Oh yes of course"*
Dan Young: *"Thanks a lot you're a sport, I'll bring it in"*
(Dan Young exits while Betty Jumel speaks to receptionist.)
Betty Jumel: *"Isn't room 257 still vacant"*
Receptionist: *"Yes it is"*
Betty Jumel; *"I thought so"*
(Nat Jackley with rouged cheeks is a 'schoolboy' dummy dressed in
striped blazer and cap his height and legs accentuated by a pair of
short trousers. Dan Young, with his hand firmly affixed to Jackley's
back walks his 'dummy' stiff legged over to the settee where they both
sit down.)

153

Betty Jumel: *"I say It's an awfully long dummy isn't it"*
Dan Young: *"Yes they're making them long these days"*
Betty Jumel: *"Why it's almost lifelike"*
Dan Young: *"Yes it is isn't it, it's wonderful"*
Betty Jumel: *"Well go on"*
Dan Young: *Go on what"?*
Betty Jumel: *"Do your stuff"*
Dan Young: *"Oh yes my stuff, my stuff"*. (To dummy): *A-ah well how are you today Tommy"?*
Nat Jackley: *"Tommy? It was George outside"*
Dan Young: *"Er, well George you mug"*
Nat Jackley: *"Well stick to your scripts"*
Dan Young: *"OK"*
Nat Jackley: (speaking of Betty Jumel) *"She's a beauty"*
Dan Young: *"That what I thought"*
Nat Jackley: *"That's hot"*
Dan Young: *"What's hot"*
Nat Jackley: *"Mustard"*
Dan Young: *"a-ha ha"*
Nat Jackley: *"it's in every shop window"*
Dan Young: *"What is"*
Nat Jackley: *"Glass"*
Dan Young: *"a-ha ha"*
Nat Jackley: *"They're two-a-penny"*
Dan Young: *"What are"*
Nat Jackley: *"Halfpennies"*
Dan Young: *"a-ha ha"*
Nat Jackley: *"It's in everybody's mouth"*
Dan Young: *"What is"*
Nat Jackley: *"Their tongue"*
(Dan Young laughs and slaps Nat Jackley on the chest, whereupon Jackley jumps up...)
Nat Jackley: *"Eh don't do that, what's the matter with you"*
Dan Young: *"Shh. Stop you fool. Sit down, sit down"*
Betty Jumel: *"I say it really is wonderful, it's mechanical as well"*
Dan Young: *"Yes. You'd be amazed what it can do"*
(Six bathing beauties enter on the way to the pool)
Dan Young: *"Am I seeing things"*
Female: *"I say girls look at the ventriloquist and his doll. What a large doll.*
(To Betty Jumel) *"If anybody phones for me will you tell them I've gone for a bathe, I won't be long.*

Betty Jumel: *"Very good miss"*
(The female attempts to fasten her shoe by lifting her leg onto the arm of the settee)
Nat Jackley: (with an eye for a shapely leg) *"Woo, Woo, pardon me, ah-lovely* (runs his fingers up her leg. At this the female turns and slaps Dan Young's face.)
Female; *"How dare you"*
Dan Young: *"Here, what's that for"*
Female: *"A liberty I call it, you ought to control your doll better than that"*
Dan Young: (To Nat Jackley) *You'll get us into trouble we'll be thrown out before we get in here"*
Nat Jackley: (Still trying to see the passing females) *"I'll screw my neck round"*
Dan Young: *"I'll screw it for you in a minute be quiet"*
(A mother with child enters)
Child: *"Ooh Mummy look at that funny man – what is it"*?
Mother: *"Hush dear it's a ventriloquist's doll"*
Dan Young: *"Correct Madam, correct"*
Child: *"What's it made of"*?
Mother: *"Wood and papier-mâché I suppose"*
Dan Young: *"You're quite right everything's wood especially the head, in fact it has no feelings at all"*
Child: *"Ooh Mummy lend me your hatpin"*
Mother: *"Hatpin - What for"*? (Mother hands pin to child)
Child: *"I want to stick it in the dummy"*
Nat Jackley: (With a look of terror) *"Hey nark it"*!
Dan Young: *"It's all right the child must play"*
Nat Jackley: *"I'm not standing for this"*
(As Nat Jackley gets up to leave, the child sticks the pin in his rear. At this, Jackley screams while Dan Young laughs, the commotion of which brings back Betty Jumel. Jackley quickly slumps back into his 'dummy' pose.)
Betty Jumel: *"You're making a lot of noise what's the matter"*?
Nat Jackley: (Through clenched teeth) *"I'll kill that kid"*
Dan Young: *"Shh"*
Betty Jumel: *"Well you've won there's a small room number 257, I'll let you have it for ten-shillings"*
Dan Young: *"Ooo you're a darling"*
Betty Jumel: *"The only thing is you won't be able to put the dummy in there"*
Dan Young: *"Why not"*?

155

Betty Jumel: *"Well it's not large enough for the two of you, but I'll put the dummy in baby's room.*
(Nat Jackley shakes his head at Dan Young in a frantic gesture of 'NO')
Dan Young: *"In baby's room...erm. Well I don't like to have the dummy out of my sight really"*
(Dan Young spots the approach of an attractive young lady)
Dan Young: *"Ooh I say who's this coming; does she live here"*
(Close-up of Nat Jackley enjoying a furtive look)
Betty Jumel: *"Yes"*
Young Lady: (To Betty Jumel) *"I'm going to my room for a lie down I don't want disturbing"*
Betty Jumel: *"All right Baby"*
Dan Young: *"Baby? Who's that?"*
Betty Jumel: *"Oh that's the manager's daughter we all call her Baby"*
The scene ends with Nat Jackley following baby up the stairs.

2:4
Over the Garden Wall – Sketch by Norman Evans

A stone is thrown over Fanny Lawton's garden wall and smashes her window. Fanny perching precariously peers over the wall.

"Who threw that through my window there. Willy Schofield I'll bat your ear'ole. You might well runaway. Good morning Mrs Jefferson I'm glad I've seen you, I was going to ask you – have you got a bit of lard you can lend me, because – I thought you hadn't – no it's – Oh it is, very scarce yes. Anyway I was – our Joe? – He's at home y'know he's pottering about in the garden. Oh he's more in the way – they are, they're better off at work are these men I've said so many a time. Well I'd made up my mind I was going out this morning – it's soon – I mean if you don't get out it's dinnertime and then you get – ooh you do, yes it's right bad. How, how are you these days? Have? Ooh I say, have you really? Well I haven't been well myself y'know because – have you – d'you mean (mouths silently). Ooh you will yes, it'll make you feel a bit worried about it; I wouldn't bother if I was you. Oooh no. Perhaps it's this 'ere bread y'know you can't tell. I – yes perhaps a bit of bicarbonate will shift it, I shouldn't worry over that because - yes, I saw your old man this morning. He's looking very well isn't he? He's what? Middle-age spread – I'll get some of that, is it on points? (Laughs at her blunder). Well y'know I haven't been well mi'self, I haven't honestly, I keep peggin' along y'know but – with me? Well no I keep erm having them hot sweats y'know. Oooh it does, it takes it out of you, y'know. These men? They don't, they don't know what it is, no. D'you know – I – well he's the same mmm... It's a funny thing y'know I was only saying last week (at this point Fanny loses her balance and smacks her ample bosom against the wall) Ouch, I say ooh that's given me a belt; that's the third time on the same brick this week y'know, I'll have to watch mi'self. How's your dog going on these days? Getting better? Our cat? Oh it's finished, oh no, it smells y'know too, mmm. It wants doin' away with – yes – it'll have to go I can smell it in the custard on Sunday. I suppose I'll have to take it, they're all soft at our house y'know. It'll be me who'll have to go t'town-hall with it y'know – yes – anyhow... Who has? Has she? Ooh – who d'you mean erm Mrs.. No I wont say a word, oh no I never talk. Well I'm not surprised I'm not a bit surprised I told her, I told her, she would go to those illuminations, I'm not a bit surprised. D'you know I never did like that coach driver. I know! He tried it on me he did that! Yes – didn't you ooh – yes – no you see it started – he started messing about with his gears. Well – hello what's that (sniffs the air)? That's my pudding ooh I forgot all about it. It's my rice pudding I left it on; it'll be burnt to a cinder, our Joe'll play little hell. Right-o I'll tell you all about it later". (Fanny slips and falls in garden pond).

Filmography.

The following filmography records detail of all the films produced by John E. Blakeley and Tom Blakeley, along with a selection of films distributed by Planet. After a fire at the Kay Film Laboratories during the early 1980s, many negatives were destroyed. Obviously, from this point on no new prints from the Mancunian films could be struck, consequently the only films available today are from surviving positive prints. The films held by Blakeley's Films today are unfortunately mostly ex-projection prints with many containing splices, cuts, scratches and bad sound. Only a few are of television broadcast quality. The London produced Butcher-Mancunian films held by the BBC have faired better and most survive in good quality versions. The British Film Institute at the National Film and Television Archive (NFTA) in London preserves some of the films and many of the extracted 'short' films are held at The North West Film Archive (NWFA) at the Manchester Metropolitan University. During the years of production John E. Blakeley's output was never accepted in the south of the country. So, is there today a place for them in a national archive? Caroline Ellis, head of Collections at the British Film Institute said, "Many regionally produced films, including those of John E. Blakeley's Mancunian Film Corporation, have a national as well as a regional significance. The Mancunian company's productions hold a key place in the British film industry. As such they deserve to be preserved for the nation in an archive with a remit to collect, preserve and make accessible to this and future generations the nation's film history". Certainly, the NFTA provides the greatest access to films than any archive in the world as is evidenced by the almost 600.000 people who saw their films during the year 2000. They also programme films for showing at the National Film Theatre and regional cinemas and at various festivals. The BFI has also released many of their holdings on VHS and DVD. Unfortunately, with over a half million titles held by the NFTA it is obvious that general access cannot be made to them all. Of course, The BFI does offer the viewing of films on their premises and this seems the only way many of the Mancunian films could be seen. However, this facility is usually only available to bona-fide students or researchers. With the Blakeley family and their Mancunian Film Corporation having been in the position as one of most successful and profitable of the country's regional film producers, perhaps an ideal situation would be to see a full collection of the surviving films being held at the North West Film Archive. As the NWFA has their emphasis focused firmly on the north of the country, maybe then the availability of the Mancunian films could become more widespread. The following titles contain both full technical and acting credits, most of which have been taken from the films themselves and/or other official sources. Where it is known that other people contributed to a film but do not have an official credit, this is noted in italics along with any relevant information. The dates given for each film are those on which the British Board of Film Classification (BBFC) granted their Certification and does not indicate the actual release date, though in most circumstances this was within a few months. It is also noted whether a film had to be cut (or not) to achieve its BBFC Certificate. A film's running time as submitted to the BBFC again does not indicate its release length, though where any significant differences occur this is noted. We have also documented where each film is archived or whether the film is one of the few that remain 'lost'. During the 1950s and 1960s, several of the Mancunian films were released onto the burgeoning 16mm collectors' market. Through the diligence of Michael Blakeley, some films that were once classed as missing have been tracked down to collectors and have now been copied. Whilst researching for this book we ourselves have also been endeavouring to trace some of the so-called 'lost' films. Having contacted many of the American Film Archives, we discovered the UCLA Film and Television Archive in California were holding a copy of 'Under New Management' (Honeymoon Hotel). After much e-mailing back and forth, they were persuaded to examine the film; especially when we explained that, it was almost certainly classed as a 'lost' picture in England. We were also eager to see what condition the film was in. The film turned out to be a 35mm acetate composite master positive (fine grain) that they had received from Paramount Pictures. All ten reels appeared to be in acceptable condition except for reel eight, which had a slight vinegar odour, indicative of beginning acetate deterioration, and the final reel, which turned out to be in a fairly advanced stage of deterioration. The UCLA then contacted Paramount with the information, and after checking their records; Paramount confirmed that they no longer had any rights in the film. They also stated that they were willing to have the fine grain repatriated to Britain if the British Film Institute wanted it. Naturally, the BFI accepted their offer stating that indeed they did very much wish to have the fine grain for their collection. The BFI is currently (2001) negotiating with Paramount for transfer of the fine grain to the NFTA, where presumably it will be further examined and copied onto

159

modern polyester stock as quickly as possible. As to the remaining 'lost' films if any film collector has any of them within their collection, please contact the authors.

Cameo Operas
Series of 12 two-reel operas
Production Company: Song Films Ltd
Producer: John E. Blakeley
Director: H. B. Parkinson (except N°10)
1: The Bohemian Girl: from the opera by William Balfe
1472ft. Cert: 'U'.
Featuring: Herbert Langley, Kathlyn Hilliard.

2: Lily of Killarney: from the opera by Charles Benedict
1690ft. Cert: 'U'.
Featuring: Herbert Langley, Kathlyn Hilliard.

3: Rigoletto: from the opera by Giuseppi Verdi.
1669ft. Cert: 'U'.
Featuring: Herbert Langley, Mme Karina, A.B. Imerson.

4: Maritana: from the opera by W.V. Wallace.
1652ft. Cert: 'U'.
Featuring: Herbert Langley, Kathlyn Hilliard.

5: Faust: from the opera by Charles Ground.
1657ft. Cert: 'U'.
Featuring: Herbert Langley, A.B. Imerson, Margot Lees.

6: Carmen: from the opera by Gorges Bizet.
1657ft. Cert: 'U'.
Featuring: Herbert Langley, Zeda Pascha.

7: La Traviata: from the opera by Giuseppi Verdi.
1605ft. Cert: 'U'.
Featuring: Anthony Ireland, Peggy Carlisle, Booth Conway.

8: Daughter of the Regiment: from the opera by Gastono Donizetti
1764ft. Cert: 'U'.
Featuring: Kitty Barling, Oscar Sosander, Algernon Hicks.

9: Martha: from the opera by Friedrich Flotow.
1608ft. Cert: 'U'
Featuring: Grizelda Hervey, Gerald Rawlinson, Algernon Hicks.

10: Il Travatore: from the opera by Giuseppi Verdi.
1130ft. Cert: 'U'.
Director: A.E. Coleby
Cast unknown.

11: The Ring: from the opera by Richard Wagner.
Two-reels (? ft) Cert: 'U'.
Cast unknown.

12: Samson and Delila: from the opera by Camille Saint-Saens.
Two-reels (? ft). Cert: 'U'.
Featuring: William Anderson.
Archive Status - All Cameo Operas are Lost, with exception of 'La Traviata' held at the NFTA

Laughter and Tears - 1928
Production Company: Song Films Ltd.
Two-reels (? ft). Cert: 'U'.
Producer: John E. Blakeley
Director: H. B. Parkinson.
Cast included Pearl Hay.
Archive Status: Lost

Two Little Drummer Boys - 1928
Production Company: Blakeley's Productions Ltd
Producer: John E. Blakeley
Director: G. B. Samuelson
Distribution: Victoria Films Ltd (London, South England, Midlands and South Wales)
Blakeley's Films (Lancashire, Yorkshire, Scotland, the four Northern Counties and Ireland)
From the stage play by Walter Howard
Studio: Southall Studios
Length 7500ft Silent
Starring Wee Georgie Wood, Derrick de Marney, Alma Taylor, Paul Cavanagh, Walter Butler, Julie Suedo, Cameron Carr and Roy Travers. *Archive Status: Lost*

Boots! Boots! - 1934
Offered to the BBFC for classification at a running time of 87m 22s
The classification of 'U' granted on 5th January was only achievable
through cuts to the film.
Length on release: 7264ft. 80mins.
Production Company: Blakeley's Productions Ltd
Distribution: Butchers
Studio: Albany Studios, Regents Park.
Marconi Visatone Sound System
Story by Jack Cottrell & George Formby*
Producer: John E. Blakeley
Director Bert Tracey
Recordist Vaughan C Sawyer
Assistant Recordist Cecil Mason
Photographed by James S Hodgson
Art Director Thomas Fleetwood
Technician Frederick G. Parsons

Music Arranged by Harry Hudson
Gowns designed and supplied by Roland & Rivkin Ltd
Starring George Formby, Beryl Formby, Arthur Kingsley, Tonie Ford.
With Lillian Keyes, Donald Reid, Constance Fletcher, Wallace Boscoe,
Betty Driver, Myfanwy Southern, Harry Hudson and his Band, *Bert
Tracey, Dan Young.*
**Though the film itself carries this acknowledgment, it would appear that the
genuine credit should go the Arthur Mertz and George Formby*
Archive Status: Held at NFTA / Blakeley Films*

Love, Mirth and Melody - 1934
Cert: No BBFC record of certificate ever being issued.
Trade shown at a length of 5856ft. 64mins
Production Company: The Mancunian Film Corporation Ltd
Registered by: Universal.
Producer: John E Blakeley
Studio: Albany Studios, Regents Park.
Marconi Visatone Sound System
Director: Bert Tracey
Story: Arthur Mertz
Flimsy story linking music hall acts. With Graham Payn, The Royal
Merry Four, Little Teddy Grey, Arthur Pond, The Lionel Claff Band,
Duggie Ascot's Dancing Girls.
Archive Status: Lost

Musical Medley -1934
Cert: No BBFC record of certificate ever being issued
Trade shown at a length of 2210ft. 25min
Production Company Mancunian Film Corporation
Registered by Universal.
Studio: Albany Studios, Regents Park.
Marconi Visatone Sound System
Produced & Directed by John E. Blakeley.
A musical review with appearances by
Lillian Keyes, Webster Booth, Master Leslie Day, Graham Payn,
Arthur Pond, Josie Santoni & Roma Clarke.
Archive Status: Lost

Off the Dole – 1935
Offered to the BBFC for classification at a running time of 96m 07s
The classification of 'A' granted on 29th March was only achievable
through cuts to the film
Length on release: 8313ft. 90mins.
Production Company: The Mancunian Film Corporation
Distributor: Associated Distributors & Producers – London, Home
and Southern Counties.
The Mancunian Film Corporation – Rest of the Country.
Studio: Albany Studios, Regents Park.
Producer John E. Blakeley
Director: Arthur Mertz
Screenplay: Arthur Mertz
Cinematographer: Sydney L. Eaton
Assistant Cameraman: Tom Blakeley
Art Director: Frank P. Atherton
Assistant Director: Herbert N. Kempley
Musical Director: Arthur L. Ward
Film Editor: Denis Cantlan
Sound: Leonard Hartley
Technician: Reginald J. Beech
Continuity: Margaret Bennet
Buckta Costumes supplied by Edward R. Buck & Sons Ltd
A Merry Musical Burlesque created by John E. Blakeley & Arthur
Mertz and Featuring: George Formby, Dan Young, Constance Shotter,
Clifford McLaglen, Beryl Formby, Tully Comber, Wally Patch. Other
Players, Stan Pell, Daisy Maynard, Stan Little, James Plant, Ken

Martin, The 16 Boy Choristers, The 12 London Babes, The Twilight Blondes, The 24 Bathing Belles, Arthur L. Ward and his Band.
Archive Status: Held at NWFA/ NFTA / Blakeley Films

Dodging the Dole – 1936
Offered to the BBFC for classification at a running time of 91m 07s
The classification of 'U' granted on 11ᵗʰ June was only achievable through cuts to the film.
Production Company: The Mancunian Film Corporation (& Distributor)
Studio: Highbury Studios, London.
Producer: John E. Blakeley
Director: John E. Blakeley.
Story: Arthur Mertz.
Cast: Roy Barbour, Dan Young, Jenny Howard, Bertha Ricardo, Hatton and Manners, The Barry Twins, The Two Jays, Steffani's Silver Songsters, Archie's Juvenile Band, Bertini and the Blackpool Tower Band.
Archive Status: Lost

The Penny Pool – 1937
Offered to the BBFC for classification at a running time of 89m 54s
The classification of 'U' granted on 2ⁿᵈ June was only achievable through cuts to the film.
Length on release: 7962ft. 84min.
Production Company: The Mancunian Film Corporation Ltd (& Distribution)
Studio: Highbury Studios, London.
RCA High Fidelity Sound System
Producer: John E. Blakeley
Director: George Black Jnr.
Cinematographer: James Burger
Camera: Louie Burger
Still Camera: Lewis Protheroe
Art Director: George Ward
Ass Art Dir: Edward Bradley
Editor: B. Bayly
Sound: A. D. Valentine
Technician: Norman Daines
Continuity: Masie Kelly
Production Manager: Charles Leeds

(Story possibly by Ronald Gow.)
Story adaptation: Arthur Mertz.
Lyrics: Arthur Mertz & Albert Stanbury.
Music: Julian Niman and his Boys.
Buckta Costumes supplied by Edward R. Buck and Sons Ltd, Manchester.
Cast: Douglas Wakefield, Billy Nelson, Chuck O'Neil, Jack Butler, Luanne Shaw, Tommy Fields. With Elsie Brown, Charles Sewell, Harry Terry, Howard Douglas, Jenny Gregson, Langley Howard, Rex Alderman, Gabrielle Brune, Helen Morant. Specialities by: Macari and his Dutch Serenaders, Marie Louise Sisters, Mascot and Morice, Fred Stilton, Jack Lewis's Singing Scholars, The 20 Gordon Ray Girls.
Archive Status: Held at NFTA / Blakeley Films

Calling All Crooks - 1938
Offered to the BBFC for classification at a running time of 93m 05s
The classification of 'A' granted on 28ᵗʰ June was only achievable through cuts to the film.
Length on release: 85mins
Production Company: The Mancunian Film Corporation (& Distribution).
Producer: John E. Blakeley.
Director. George Black Jnr.
Story: Arthur Mertz.
Cinematographer: Desmond Dickinson
Cast: Douglas Wakefield, Billy Nelson, Leslie Perrins, Helen Barnes, Chuck O'Neil, Jack Butler, Dan Young, Howard Rogers, Raymond Smith, Seven Royal Hindustanis, Velda & Vann, Hal Wright and his Circus, Sixty Sherman Fisher Girls, Ten Master Singers, Thirty Gypsy Revellers.
Archive Status: Lost

Somewhere in England – 1940
Offered to the BBFC for classification at a running time of 79m 13s
The classification of 'A' granted on 30ᵗʰ July was only achievable through cuts to the film.
Production Company: Butcher-Mancunian.
Distribution: Butchers Film Services.

Studio: Walton-on-Thames
RCA Photophone Sound System
Producer: John E. Blakeley
Director: John E. Blakeley.
Story: Roney Parsons
Screen Adaptation: Anthony Toner
Cinematographer: Geoffrey Faithfull.

166

Art Director: R. Holmes Paul
Editor: E. Richards
Production Manager: C. Sanderson
Sound: Hal Fuller
Assistant Director: Cecil Dixon
Musical Director: Percival Mackey
Music: Albert W. Stanbury
Lyrics: Arthur Mertz
Orchestrations: Hal Bevan & Oscar Naylor
Cast: Harry Korris, Frank Randle, Winki Turner, Dan Young, Robbie
Vincent, Harry Kemble, John Singer, Sidney Monkton, Stanley King,
8 Master Singers, Percival Mackey's Orchestra.
Archive Status: Held at NFTA

Somewhere in Camp – 1942
Offered to the BBFC for classification at a running time of 88m 19s
The classification of 'U' granted on 27th January was achieved with no
cuts to the film.
Production Company: Butcher-Mancunian.
Distribution: Butchers Film Service
Studio: Riverside Studios.
RCA Photophone Sound System
Producer: John E. Blakeley
Director: John E. Blakeley
Story: Roney Parsons and Anthony Toner.
Cinematographer: Stephen Dade.
Art Director: W. Hemsley.
Editor: A. C. Knott.
Production Manager: E. S. Laurie.
Sound: George Burgess.
Ass Director: W. Boyle.
Lyrics: Arthur Mertz.
Music: A. W. Stanbury.
Percival Mackey and his Orchestra.
Cast: Harry Korris, Frank Randle, Robbie Vincent, Dan Young, Tonie
Lupino, John Singer, *(Peggy Novak, Clifford Buckton, Gus Aubrey, Betty
Wheatly, Eve Carcroft)*.
*Archive Status: Held at BBC**

Somewhere on Leave – 1942
Offered to the BBFC for classification at a running time of 96m 07s
The classification of 'U' granted on 14ᵗʰ October was achieved with no
cuts to the film.
Production Company: Butcher-Mancunian.
Distribution: Butchers Film Service
Studio: Riverside Studios.
RCA Photophone Sound System
Producer: John E. Blakeley
Director: John E. Blakeley
Story: Roney Parsons and Anthony Toner.
Cinematographer: Geoffrey Faithfull.
Art Director: W. J. Hemsley.
Editor: E. Richards
Production Manager: E. S. Laurie.
Sound: George Burgess and S. Jolly.
Ass Director: D. Weeks.
Lyrics: Arthur Mertz.
Percival Mackey and his Orchestra.
Cast: Frank Randle, Harry Korris, Dan Young, Robbie Vincent, Tonie
Lupino, Pat McGrath, Tonie Edgar Bruce. *(Noel Dainton, Gus Aubrey)*.
Archive Status: Held at BBC*

Demobbed – 1944
Offered to the BBFC for classification at a running time of 95m 33s
The classification of 'U' granted on 24ᵗʰ April was only achievable
through cuts to the film.
Production Company: Butcher-Mancunian.
Distribution: Butchers Film Service.
Studio: Riverside Studios, London.
RCA Photophone Sound System
Producer: John E. Blakeley.
Director: John E. Blakeley.
Story: Roney Parsons and Anthony Toner.
Cinematographer: Geoffrey Faithfull and G. Gibbs.
Art Dir: Jim Carter
Editor: Ted Richards.
Production Manager: E. S. Laurie.
Sound: George Burgess and S. Jolly.
Camera: A. Mason
Ass Director: D. Weeks

Musical Director: Percival Mackey.
Comedy Sequences: Arthur Mertz.
Cast: Norman Evans, Nat Jackley, Dan Young, Betty Jumel, Tony Dalton, James Plant, George Merritt, Fred Kitchen, Arthur Hambling, Gus McNaughton, Marianne Lincoln, Anne Firth, Neville Mapp. Guest artistes: Webster Booth and Anne Ziegler. Special Hawaiian Scena: Felix Mendelssohn's Hawaiian Serenaders.
Archive Status: Held at BBC/ NFTA*

Home Sweet Home - 1945
Offered to the BBFC for classification at a running time of 93m 31s
The classification of 'A' granted on 11ᵗʰ July was only achievable through cuts to the film.
Production Company: Butcher-Mancunian.
Distribution: Butchers Film Service
Studio: Riverside Studios
RCA Photophone Sound System
Producer: John E. Blakeley.
Director: John E. Blakeley.
Story: Roney Parsons and Anthony Toner.
Comedy scenes devised & arranged by Arthur Mertz
Cinematographer: Geoffrey.
Camera: A. Mason
Art Director: Jim Carter
Editor V Sagovsky
Sound: G. Burgess & L. Clark
Production Manager: E. S. Laurie
Assistant Director: Don Weeks
Musical Director: Percival Mackey
Starring Frank Randle. Introducing as Guest Artistes Rawicz & Landauer. With Nicolette Roeg, Tony Pendrell, H.F. Maltby, Hilda Bayley, Cecil Frederick, Stan Little, Donovan & Byl, Arnley & Gloria, Bunty Meadows. Special Musical Ensembles by Percival Mackey – Soloist Helen Hill
*Archive Status: Held at BBC**

Under New Management – 1945
Offered to the BBFC for classification at a running time of 91m
The classification of 'A' granted on 31ˢᵗ December was achieved with no cuts to the film.
Re-submitted as Honeymoon Hotel to the BBFC for classification in 1948.

The Classification of 'A' granted on 27th January was achieved with no cuts to the film.
Production Company: Butcher-Mancunian.
Distribution: Butchers Film Service.
Studio: Riverside Studios
RCA Photophone Sound System
Producer: John E. Blakeley
Director: John E. Blakeley
Story and Scenario: Roney Parsons and Anthony Toner
Cinematographer: Geoffrey Faithfull
Art Director: Jim Carter
Editor: V. Sagovsky
Production Manager: E. S. Laurie
Sound: G. Burgess and H. C. Pearson
Camera: A. Mason
Assistant Director: Don Weeks
Musical Director: Percival Mackey
Comedy Sequences: Arthur Mertz
Special Musical Numbers by Albert Stanbury and Arthur Mertz
Cast: Norman Evans, Nat Jackley, Dan Young, Betty Jumel, Nicolette Roeg, Marianne Lincoln, Bunty Meadows, Michael Taylor, Aubrey Mallalieu, George Mulcaster, Tony Dalton, John Rorke, Barbara Valerie, Hay Petrie, Lily Lapidus, Gordon McLeod, Joss Ambler, David Keir, John Allen, Dick Beamish, Arthur Vollum, Cavan O'Connor, Marcel Vallèe, Andre Genin, Jaques Varennes, Lynda Ross, The Donovan Octette, Mendel's Female Sextette, Percival Mackey's Orchestra.
Archive Status: Originally held at UCLA Film and Television Archive, California, USA, transferring to the NFTA, London during 2001.

(*All enquiries relating to copyright or exploitation of the Butcher's Library titles should be referred to Programme Acquisitions, BBC TV London)

Cup-Tie Honeymoon – 1947
Offered to the BBFC for classification at a running time of 91m 40s
The classification of 'A' granted on 1st December was only achievable through cuts to the film.
Production Company: Film Studios (Manchester) Ltd.
Distribution: The Mancunian Film Corporation.
Studio: Film Studios Manchester.

Marconi Visatone Sound System.
Producer: John E. Blakeley.
Director: John E. Blakeley.
Story: Roney Parsons and Anthony Toner, *(Harry Jackson)*.
Cinematographer: Geoffrey Faithfull.
Camera: Gerald Pullen
Sound: Kenneth Ross and W. Howell
Editor: Dorothy Stimson
Continuity: Joyce Bedale
Art Dir: Joseph Gomersall
Studio Manager: Bernard Kelly
Lyrics: A. W. Stanbury
Musical Dir: Fred Harris
Gowns: Lynda Gay, Manchester
Set Decoration: Pauldens Ltd, Manchester
Cast: Sandy Powell, Dan Young, Betty Jumel, Pat McGrath, Joyanne Bracewell, Violet Farebrother, Bruce Carstairs, Hilary Dean, David Carey, Lola Derrol, Frank Groves, Mavis Compston, Patricia Pilkington, Barbara McClelland, Vic Arnley, Howard Douglas.
Archive Status: Held with Blakeley's Films

Holiday's with Pay - 1948
Offered to the BBFC for classification at a running time of 113m 45s
The classification of 'A' granted on 1ˣ March was achieved with no cuts to the film.
Production Company: Film Studios (Manchester) Ltd
Distribution: The Mancunian Film Corporation
Studio: Film Studios Manchester
Marconi Visatone Sound System
Producer: John E. Blakeley
Director: John E. Blakeley
Story: Anthony Toner
Screen Adaptation: Harry Jackson and Mavis Compston
Cinematographer: Ben Hart
Camera: Gerald Pullen, John E. Blakeley Jnr
Sound: Kenneth Ross
Editor: Dorothy Stimson
Continuity: Joyce Bedale
Art Director: Joseph Gomersall
Production Manager: Bernard Kelly
Make-up: Victor Arnley

171

Hair Stylist: Ann Reynolds
Casting Director: Arthur Mertz Jnr.
Assistant Director: Thomas Blakeley
Lyrics: Albert W. Stanbury
Musical Director: Fred Harris
Furnishings by Pauldens Ltd Manchester
Cast: Frank Randle, Tessie O'Shea, Dan Young, Josef Locke with
Sally Barnes, Sonny Burke, Joanne Bracewell, Effie Mackintosh, Peter
Lilley, Rita Varian, Rita Young, Danny Young, Bert Tracey, Patrina
Bowman
Archive Status: Held with Blakeley's Films

Somewhere in Politics – 1948
Offered to the BBFC for classification
at a running time of 110m
The classification of 'A' granted on 13th
October was achieved with no cuts.
Length on release: 9700ft. 108mins.
Production Company:
Film Studios (Manchester) Ltd
Distribution:
The Mancunian Film Corporation
Studio: Film Studios Manchester
Marconi Visatone Sound System
Producer: John E. Blakeley.
Director: John E. Blakeley.
Story: Harry Jackson, Arthur Mertz,
and Frank Randle
Cinematographer: Ernest Palmer
and Ben Hart
Editor: Dorothy Stimson
Art Dir: Joseph Gomersall
Musical Arrangements:
Fred Harris and Fred Bonelli
Cast: Frank Randle, Tessie
O'Shea, Josef Locke, Syd & Max
Harrison, Sally Barnes, Jimmy

Clitheroe, Bunty Meadows, Sonny Burke, Anthony Oakley, Effie
Macintosh, Kay Compston, Bernard Graham, Fred Simister, George Little.
Archive Status: Lost (see extracts section – 'Full House')

172

International Circus Review – 1948
Offered to the BBFC for classification at a running time of 52m 47s
The classification of 'U' granted on 9th September was achieved with
no cuts to the film.
Production Company: Film Studios (Manchester) Ltd
Distribution: The Mancunian Film Corporation
Filmed on location at BelleVue Circus, Manchester
Sound System: Not Stated
Producer: Tom Blakely
Director: Tom Blakeley
Cinematographer: Gerald Pullen, John E. Blakeley Jnr.
Editor: Dorothy Stimson
Featuring: Madame Michaela Constance, Gilbert Houke & Royal
Bengal Tigers, The Amazing Kovaks, The Three Austins, Tarzan and
Pongo, Tagora and Partner, Colls Chimps, Adamskis Bears, Sam
Linfield and Company, The Les Rays Skating Typhoons, Musical
Derricks and Tony.
Archive Status: Held with NWFA

Showground of the North – 1948
Offered to the BBFC for classification at a running time of 33m 59s
The classification of 'U' granted on 20ᵗʰ July was achieved with no cuts
to the film.
Production Company: Film Studios (Manchester) Ltd
Distribution: The Mancunian Film Corporation
Filmed on location at BelleVue Zoological Gardens, Manchester
Sound System: Not Stated
Producer: Tom Blakeley
Cinematographer: Gerald Pullen, John E. Blakeley Jnr.
Editor: Dorothy Stimson
Commentary Writer: Mavis Compton
Narrator: Lionel Marsden
Archive Status: Lost

What-a-Carry-On! - 1949
Offered to the BBFC for classification at a running time of 93m 22s
The classification of 'U' granted on 22ⁿᵈ August was only achievable
through cuts to the film
Production Company: Film Studios (Manchester) Ltd
Distribution: The Mancunian Film Corporation.
Studio: Film Studios Manchester

Sound System: British Acoustic Film System
Producer: John E. Blakeley
Director: John E. Blakeley
Story: Anthony Toner
Screen Adaptation: Harry Jackson
Cinematographer: Ernest Palmer
Camera: Hal Britton
Sound: Michael Hobbs
Editor: Dorothy Stimson
Continuity: Doris Martin
Art Director: Joseph Gomersall
Production Manager: Bernard Kelly
Make-up: John Webber
Musical Director: Fred Harris
Assistant Director: Tom Blakeley
Cast: Jimmy Jewel, Ben Warriss, Josef Locke, Shirley Quenten, Tony Pendrell, Terry Randall, Anthony Oakley, Eve Eacot, Ian Fleming, Stanley Van Beers, Langley Howard, Patrick Baring, Kitty Bluett
Archive Status: Held with Blakeley's Films

School for Randle - 1949
Offered to the BBFC for classification at a running time of 89m 13s
The classification of 'U' granted on 4ᵗʰ November was achieved with no cuts to the film
Production Company: Film Studios (Manchester) Ltd
Distribution: The Mancunian Film Corporation
Studio: Film Studios Manchester
Sound System: British Acoustic Film System
Producer: John E. Blakeley
Director: John E. Blakeley
Story: Anthony Toner
Screen Adaptation: Harry Jackson
Cinematographer: Ernest Palmer
Sound: Michael Hobbs
Editor: Dorothy Stimson
Continuity: Doris Martin
Art Director: Joseph Gomersall
Make-up: Harry Webber
Musical Director: Billy Butler
Assistant Director: Tom Blakeley
Studio Manager: Bernard Kelly

Cast: Frank Randle, John Singer, Elsa Tee, Frederick Bradshaw, Dan Young, Alec Pleon, Maudie Edwards, Hilda Bayley, Ian Fleming, Jimmy Clitheroe, Joan Henley, *Gus Aubrey*
Archive Status: Held with Blakeley's Films

Over the Garden Wall – 1950
Offered to the BBFC for classification at an undetermined length. The classification of 'U' granted on 13ᵗʰ March was only achievable through cuts to the film
Length on release: 94mins
Production Company: Film Studios (Manchester) Ltd
Distribution: The Mancunian Film Corporation
New Realm (South England)
Studio: Film Studios Manchester
Sound System: British Acoustic Film System
Producer: John E. Blakeley
Director: John E. Blakeley
Story: Anthony Toner
Screen Adaptation: Harry Jackson
Cinematographer: Ernest Palmer
Camera: John E. Blakeley Jnr.
Sound: Michael Hobbs
Art Director: Joseph Gomersall
Editor: Dorothy Stimson
Continuity: Doris Martin
Make-up: John Webber
Musical Director: Billy Butler
Assistant Director: Tom Blakeley
Cast: Norman Evans, Jimmy James, Dan Young, Alec Pleon, Sonya O'Shea, Frederick Bradshaw, Agnes Bernelle, John Wynn, Neville Brook, Patrick Baring, Langley Howard, Peter Broadbent, Billy Howard, *Eli Woods.*
Archive Status: Held with NFTA/Blakeley's Films

Lets Have a Murder – 1950
Offered to the BBFC for classification at a running time of 108m 53s
The classification of 'U' granted on 5ᵗʰ July was achieved with no cuts to the film
Length on release: 95mins
Production Company: Film Studios (Manchester) Ltd
Distribution: The Mancunian Film Corporation

Studio: Film Studios Manchester
Sound System: British Acoustic Film System
Producer: John E. Blakeley
Director: John E. Blakeley
Story: Anthony Toner
Cinematographer: Ernest Palmer
Camera Operator: John E. Blakeley Jnr.
Sound: Michael Hobbs
Continuity: Gladys Goldsmith
Editor: Dorothy Stimson
Art Director: Joe Gomersall
Make-up: Harry Webber
Musical Director: Billy Butler
Production Manager: Tom Blakeley
Cast: Jimmy Jewell, Ben Warriss, David Greene, June Elvin, Lesley
Osmond, Stewart Rome, Ruth Taylor, Agnes Burnelle, Peter Forbes
Robertson, Denis Val Norton, Michael Ripper, Arthur White,
Cameron Hall, David Josephs, Jack Hayes, *Kitty Bluett, Claude Dampier,
Anthony Pendrell, Eva Eacot.* Musical Speciality number by Betty Paul
Archive Status: Lost (see extracts section – 'Stick 'em Up')

Loves a Luxury – 1952
(US title – The Caretaker's Daughter)
Cert: 'A' 7613ft. 89mins.
Production Company: Film Studios (Manchester) Ltd
Distribution: The Mancunian Film Corporation
Studio: Film Studios Manchester
Sound System: G. B. Kalee Recording
Producer: Tom Blakeley
Director: Francis Searle
Story: (Play) Guy Paxton, Edward V. Hoile
Screen Adaptation: Francis Searle, Elwyn Ambrose
Cinematographer: Ernest Palmer
Camera: Herbert Mason
Production Manager: Bernard Kelly
Art Director: Joseph Gomersall
Editor: Dorothy Stimson
Sound: H. P. Pearson
Make-up: Peter Evans
Hairdresser: Barbra Horobin
Continuity: Gladys Goldsmith

Ass Director: A. Marotta
Wardrobe: Betty Adamson
Still Cameraman: Deryk Whittaker
Music Arranged by: Harry Pedlar
Cast: Hugh Wakefield, Derek Bond, Michael Medwin, Helen Shingler, Zena Marshall, Patricia Raine, Bill Shine, Grace Arnold
Archive Status: Held with NWFA/NFTA/Blakeley's Films

Those People Next Door – 1952
Offered as Wearing the Pants to the BBFC for classification at an undetermined length
The classification of 'U' granted on 8th August was only achievable through cuts to the film
Re-offered as Those People Next Door for classification at an undetermined length
The classification of 'U' granted on 14th August was only achievable through cuts to the film
Length on release: 77mins.
Production Company: Film Studios (Manchester) Ltd
Distribution: Eros
Studio: Film Studios Manchester
Sound System: Gaumont British Kalee
Producer: Tom Blakeley
Director: John Harlow
Story. Zelda Davees from her stage play 'Wearing the Pants'
Cinematographer: Roy Fogwell
Editor: Dorothy Stimson
Cast: Jack Warner, Marjorie Rhodes, Charles Victor, Garry Marsh, Jimmy James, Patricia Cutts, Peter Forbes-Robertson, Anthony Newley, Gladys Henson, Norah Gaaussen, Grace Arnold, Geoffrey Sumner
Archive Status: Lost – though it is thought prints survive in the hands of private collectors

Elephants Come To Town – 1953
Offered to the BBFC for classification at a running time of 36m 40s
The classification of 'U' granted on 13th March was achieved with no cuts to the film
Length on release: 33mins
Production Company: Film Studios (Manchester) Ltd
Distribution: The Mancunian Film Corporation

Filmed on Location
Producer: Tom Blakeley
Director: Tom Blakely
Editor: Dorothy Stimson
Commentary by Lionel Marsden
Circus 'short' featuring Chipperfield's Travelling Circus
Archive Status: Held at NWFA

It's a Grand Life – 1953
Offered to the BBFC for classification at a running time of 106m 40s
The classification of 'U' granted on 8th October was only achievable
through cuts to the film.
Length on release: 102mins
Production Company: Film Studios (Manchester) Ltd
Distribution: The Mancunian Film Corporation
Studio: Film Studios Manchester
Sound System: Gaumont British Kalee
Producer: John E. Blakeley
Director: John E. Blakeley
Story: H. F. Maltby
Cinematographer: Ernest Palmer
Sound: David Howells
Editor: Dorothy Stimson
Continuity: Gladys Goldsmith
Art Dir: Alec Gray
Assistant Dir: Bert Marotta
Make-up: Gerry Fairbank
Production Manager: Tom Blakeley
Cast: Frank Randle, Diana Dors, Dan Young, Michael Brennan,
Jennifer Jayne, John Blythe, Anthony Hulme, Charles Peters, Arthur
White, Leslie Gould, Kevin Peters, Ian Fleming, Ruth Taylor.
Appearances by championship wrestlers: Jack Pye, Bill Garnon, Cab
Cashford, Carl Van Wurden. Special Guest Artiste Winifred Atwell
Archive Status: Held with Blakeley's Films

Lovely Weekend - 1956
Offered to the BBFC for classification at a running time of 29m 27s
The classification of 'U' granted on 17th May was achieved with no cuts
to the film.
Colour
Production Company: Mancunian

Distributor: Rank1958
Shot on location in Cheshire
Produced and Directed by Tom Blakeley
Photography by John E Blakeley Jnr
Edited by Dorothy Stimson
Original story by Anthony Toner
Camera Assistant David Wood
Cast: Jane Peters, Deirdre Clear, Marlene Nelson
Archive Status: Held with NWFA

Trouble with Eve - 1959
(US Title – In Trouble with Eve)
Originally offered to the BBFC for classification as In Walked Eve at
a running time of 66m 13s. The classification of 'U' granted on 3rd
November was achieved with no cuts to the film.
Re-offered to the BBFC for classification as Trouble with Eve at a
running time of 66m 13s
The classification of 'U' granted on 8th September 1960 was achieved
with no cuts to the film
Production Company: Blakeley's Films (Manchester) Ltd
Distribution: Butcher's Film Distributors
Studio: Walton Studios
RCA Sound System
Producer: Tom Blakeley.
Assistant Producer: John E. Blakeley Jnr.
Director: Francis Searle
Screen Play: Brock Williams
From stage play 'Widows are Dangerous' by June Garland
Cinematographer: James Harvey
Camera: David Mason
Sound: Syd Wyles
Assistant Director: Roger Marley
Make-up: Jimmy Hydes
Editor: Eric Boyd Perkins
Art Director: John Earl
Production Manager: Charles Leeds
Continuity: Leonora Hayles
Music: Wilfred Burns

Cast: Robert Urquhart, Hy Hazell, Garry Marsh, Vera Day, Sally Smith, Tony Quinn, Brenda Hogan, Denis Shaw, Grace Denbeigh-Russell, Bill Shine, Bruce Seton, Iris Vandeleur, Frank Atkinson
Archive Status: Held with NFTA/Blakeley's Films

Rag Doll - 1960
(US Title - Young, Willing and Eager)
Offered to the BBFC for classification at a running time of 66m 07s
The classification of 'A' granted on 29th December was only achievable through cuts to the film
Production Company: Blakeley's Films (Manchester) Ltd
Distribution: Butcher's Film Distributors.
Studio: Walton Studios
RCA Sound System
Producer: Tom Blakeley
Director: Lance Comfort
Story: Brock Williams
Screenplay: Brock Williams, Derry Quinn
Cinematographer: Basil Emmott
Sound: William Buckley
Editor: Peter Pitt
Art Director: John Earl
Continuity: Marjorie Lavelly
Music: Martin Slavin
Lyrics: Abbe Gail
Costumes: Dulcie Midwinter
Cast: Jess Conrad, Hermione Baddeley, Kenneth Griffith, Christina Gregg, Patrick Magee, Michael Wayne, Patrick Jordan, Frank Forsyth, Marie Devereux, Eve Eden, Frank Hawkins, Linda Castle
Archive Status: Held with NFTA/Blakeley's Films

Painted Smile - 1961
(US Title - Murder Can Be Deadly)
Offered to the BBFC for classification at a running time of 61m 40s
The classification of 'A' granted on 14th September was only achievable through cuts to the film
Production Company: Blakeley's Films (Manchester) Ltd
Distribution: Planet
Studio: Shepperton Studios
Westrex Recording System
Producer: Tom Blakeley

Director: Lance Comfort.
Story Idea: Brock Williams
Screenplay: Pip and Jane Baker
Cinematographer: Basil Emmott
Camera: Frank Drake
Sound: Norman Bolland
Editor: John Trumper
Art Director: George Provis
Continuity: Phyllis Townshend
Assistant Director: Peter Price
Production Manager: Pat Green
Music Director: Martin Slavin
Songs: 'Another You', Composer Norrie Paramor, Lyrics Bunny Lewis
& Michael Carr. 'Painted Smile', Composer Martin Slavin, Lyrics
Abbe Gail. Singer: Craig Douglas.
Hairdresser: Bobbie Smith
Wardrobe: Maude Churchill
Cast: Liz Fraser, Kenneth Griffith, Peter Reynolds, Tony Wickert,
Craig Douglas, Nanette Newman, Ray Smith, David Hemmings,
Harold Berens, Grazina Frame, Richard McNeff, Gerald Sim,
Rosemary Chalmers, Mia Karam, Terry Maidment, Bill Stevens,
Lionel Ngakane, Ann Wrigg
Archive Status: Held with NFTA/Blakeley's Films

The Break – 1962
Offered to the BBFC for classification at a running time of 76m 47s
The classification of 'A' granted on 16th March was only achievable
through cuts to the film
Production Company: Mancunian Film Corporation
Distribution: Planet
Studio: Shepperton Studios
Westrex Recording System
Producer: Tom Blakeley
Director: Lance Comfort.
Screenplay: Pip and Jane Baker
Cinematographer: Basil Emmott
Camera: Frank Drake
Sound: Buster Ambler
Editor: Peter Pitt
Assistant Director: Roy Baird
Art Director: George Provis

Continuity: Jane Buck
Hairdresser: Bobbie Smith
Make-up: Freddy Williamson
Wardrobe: Jean Fairlie
Production Manager: John Comfort
Music Director: Brian Fahey
Cast: Tony Britton, William Lucas, Eddie Byrne, Robert Urquhart, Sonia Dresdel, Edwin Richfield, Gene Anderson, Christina Gregg, Patrick Jordan, John Junkin, Marshall Jones
Archive Status: Held with NFTA/Blakeley's Films

Tomorrow at Ten – 1962
Offered to the BBFC for classification at a running time of 80m 02s
The classification of 'A' granted on 21ˢ September was only achievable through cuts to the film
Production Company: Mancunian Film Corporation
Distribution: Planet
Studio: MGM Studios, Borehamwood
Westrex Recording System
Producer: Tom Blakeley
Director: Lance Comfort
Story & Screenplay: James Kelly & Peter Miller
Cinematographer: Basil Emmott
Camera: Frank Drake
Sound: Fred Turtle
Editor: Peter Pitt
Assistant Editor: Peter Murton
Production Manager: John Comfort
Music Director: Bernie Fenton
Assistant Director: George Pollard
Art Director: Jack Shampan
Continuity: Phyllis Townshend
Make-up: Peter Armston
Wardrobe: Bob Rayner
Property Buyer: Bill Isaacs
Cast: John Gregson, Robert Shaw, Alec Clunes, Alan Wheatley, Kenneth Cope, Ernest Clarke, Piers Bishop, Harry Fowler, Renee Houston, Noel Howlett, Bernadette Woodman, Marguerite McCourt, Ray Smith, John Dunbar, Edward Rees, Anthony Ashdown, Kenneth Gilbert, Norman Coburn, Norman Hartley, Stephen Mayling, Peter Mason, Frank Hawkins, Christopher Ellis, Robert Hunter, Trevor

Reid, Neville Taylor, Lesley Allen. Guest Stars: Helen Cherry, William Hartnell, Betty McDowell
Archive Status: Held with NFTA/Blakeley's Films

The Marked One – 1963
Offered to the BBFC for classification at a running time of 64m 43s
The classification of 'A' granted on 31ˢᵗ May was achieved with no cuts to the film
Production Company: Planet Film Productions
Distribution: Planet Film Distributors
Producer: Tom Blakeley
Production Manager: Clive Midwinter
Director: Francis Searle
Assistant Director: Stuart Freeman
Screenplay: Paul Erickson
Cinematographer: Frank Kingston, Frank Patten
Sound: David Bowen
Cast: William Lucas, Zena Walker, Patrick Jordan, Laurie Leigh, David Gregory, Edward Ogden, Arthur Lovegrove, Brian Nisson, Kim Tracey, Marianne stone, Richard McNeff, Frank Sieman, Lyn Pinkney, Candy Pibworth, Gillian watt, Gordon Wayne, Philip Ross, Tex Fuller, Jack Taylor, June Sylvaine, Dorothy Gordon, Frederick Peisley, Margaret Flint, John Watson
Archive Status: Held with Blakeley's Films

Blind Corner – 1963
(US title – Man in the Dark)
Offered to the BBFC for classification at an unmeasured length
The classification of 'A' granted on 5ᵗʰ November was only achievable through cuts to the film
Production Company: Mancunian Film Corporation
Distributor: Planet
Length of release: 7198ft. 80mins
Studio: Pinewood Studios
Westrex Recording System
Producer: Tom Blakeley
Director: Lance Comfort
Production Manager: John Comfort
Production Secretary: Ann Skinner
Continuity: Lorely Farley
Assistant Director: John Stoneman

Screenplay: James Kelly & Peter Miller
Based on a story by Vivian Kemble
Cinematographer: Basil Emmott
Editor: John Trumper
Assistant editor: Roy Taylor
Art Director: John St. John Earl
Sound: Robert McPhee
Make-up: George Blackler
Hairdresser: Ann Box
Wardrobe: Eve Faloon
Musical Director: Brian Fahey
Musical Advisor: Frank Patten
Cast: William Sylvester, Barbara Shelley, Elizabeth Shepherd, Alex Davion, Mark Eden, Ronnie Carroll, Barry Aldis, Edward Evans, Frank Forsyth
Archive Status: Held with NFTA/Blakeley's Films

Devils of Darkness – 1964
Offered to the BBFC for classification at a running time of 88m 11s
The classification of 'X' granted on 1ˢᵗ July was only achievable through cuts to the film
Production Company: Planet Film Productions
Distributor: Planet Film Distributors
Eastman Colour
Studio: Pinewood Studios
Westrex Recording System
Producer: Tom Blakeley
Director: Lance Comfort
Production Manager: John Comfort
Continuity: Muire Mathieson
Assistant Director: Roy Baird
Screenplay: Lyn Fairhurst
Cinematographer: Reginald Wyer
Editor: John Trumper
Art Director: John St. John Earl
Sound: Robert McPhee, Gordon McCallum
Music: Bernie Fenton
Choreographer: Leo Kharibian
Costumes: Muriel Dickson
Cast: William Sylvester, Hubert Noel, Tracey Reed, Carol Gray, Rona Anderson, Peter Illing, Avril Angers, Eddie Byrne, Diana Decker,

Gerald Heinz, Marianne Stone, Victor Brooks, Brian Oulton, Marie Burke, Olwen Brookes, Geoffrey Kenion, Rod McLennan, Burnell Tucker, Julie Mendes

Island of Terror – 1966
Offered to the BBFC for classification at a running time of 84m 07s
The classification of 'X' granted on 4th February was only achievable through cuts to the film
Production Company: Planet Film Productions
Distributor: Planet Film Distributors
Eastman Colour
Studio: Pinewood Studios
Westrex Recording System
Producer: Tom Blakeley
Director: Terence Fisher
Production Manager: Roy Baird
Continuity: Kay Mander
Assistant Director: Don Weeks
Camera: Frank Drake
Story & Screenplay: Edward Andrew Mann and Alan Ramsen
Cinematographer: Reginald Wyer
Editor: Thelma Connell
Art Director: John St. John Earl
Assistant Art Director: Fred Hole
Sound: Robert McPhee, Gordon McCallum
Music: Malcolm Lockyer - Electronic Effects: Barry Gray
Wardrobe: Rosemary Burrows
Make-up: Bunty Phillip
Hairdresser: Stella Rivers
Special Effects/Make-up artiste: Billy Partleton
Special effects created by John St. John Earl assisted by Michael Albrechtson
Cast: Peter Cushing, Edward Judd, Carole Gray, Eddie Byrne, Sam Kydd, Nial MacGinnis, James Caffrey, Liam Gaffney, Roger Heathcote, Keith Bell, Margaret Lacy, Shay Gorman, Peter Forbes Robertson, Richard Bidlake, Joyce Hemson, Edward Ogden

The Night of the Big Heat – 1967
(US title – Island of the Burning Doomed/ Island of the Burning Damned)
Offered to the BBFC for classification at a running time of 92m 17s

185

The classification of 'X' granted on 4ᵗʰ May was achieved with no cuts to the film
Production Company: Planet Film Productions
Distributor: Planet Film Distributors
Eastman Colour
Studio: Pinewood Studios
Westrex Recording System
Producer: Tom Blakeley
Director: Terence Fisher
Screenplay: Pip barker, Jane Barker, Rob Liles
From the novel by John Lymington
Cinematographer: Reginald Wyer
Editor: Rod Keys
Art Director: Alex Vetchinsky
Wardrobe: Kathleen Moore
Sound: Dudley Messenger, E. Karnon
Music: Malcolm Lockyer
Cast: Christopher Lee, Patrick Allen, Peter Cushing, Jane Merrow, Sarah Lawson, William Lucas, Kenneth Cope, Percy Herbert, Tony Heathcote, Anna Turner, Jack Bligh, Sidney Bromley, Barry Halliday.

Short extract subjects.

Music Hall Personalities
Series of 'shorts' edited from various Blakeley Features. All Cert U.

N° 1: includes footage from *Dodging the Dole*. 1548ft. Released 1938.
N°2: George Formby: includes footage from *Off the Dole*. 1436ft. Released 1938
N° 3: includes footage from *Dodging the Dole*. 1738ft. Released 1938.
N° 4: George Formby: includes footage from *Boots! Boots!* 2052ft. Released 1938
N° 5: includes footage from *Off the Dole*. 1682ft. Released 1938
N° 6: George Formby: includes footage from *Off the Dole*. 1793ft. Released 1938
N° 7: (1521ft), 8: (1640ft), 9: (1459ft), 10: (1632ft), 11: (1615ft), 12: (1626ft) all include footage from *The Penny Pool*. Released 1939
N° 13: (1619ft), 14: (1849ft), 15: (1705ft), 16: (1539ft), 17: (1630ft), 18: (1536ft) all include footage from *Calling all Crooks*. N°14: also includes footage from *Love, Mirth and Melody*. Released 1940
Archive Status: Lost.

The Song that Made a Star. Cert U
This film has George Formby singing six songs extracted from both
'Boots! Boots! and *'Off the Dole'*. Beryl Formby is also seen performing
her dance routine to the music of Chinese Laundry Blues. The film
was introduced to cinemagoers with the following caption card "*It must
be of great interest to cinema audiences to hear once again the songs that proved
to be the stepping-stones to stardom of a great artist. So here is what may be
termed 'A Cavalcade of Song' the numbers that raised to fame the one and only
George Formby - The Idol Of The People".* Released circa 1938
Archive Status: Held with Blakeley's Films.

With the following films the title that appears in brackets is the film
from which the under mentioned 'shorts' were extracted. The dates
used are those on which the BBFC granted certification.

(Home Sweet Home)
Randle and All That – 7ᵗʰ December 1945
Cert: A (with cuts)
Archive Status: Held by the BBC

(Holidays with Pay)
Tonight's The Nite – 2ⁿᵈ June 1960
1672ft. Cert U (uncut).
Seaside Frolics – 2ⁿᵈ June 1960
1700ft. 18mins. Cert U (uncut).
Archive Status: Held at the NWFA.

(Somewhere in Politics)
Full House – 2ⁿᵈ June 1960
1700ft. 18mins Cert U (uncut).
Archive Status: Held at the NWFA.

(What-a-Carry-On!)
Joining the Army - 13ᵗʰ November 1952
1600ft Cert U (uncut).
Sergeant's Pets – 5ᵗʰ February 1959
1600ft. Cert U (uncut).

Army Capers – 5ᵗʰ February 1959
1600ft. Cert U (uncut).
Archive Status: Held at the NWFA.

(School for Randle)
Teacher's Pest – 4th February 1960
4200ft. 46mins. Cert U (uncut)
The Three Who-Flungs – 4th February 1950
1200ft. Cert U (uncut).
Bella's Birthday – 29th August 1950
1387ft. 15mins. Cert U (with cuts)
Archive Status: Held at the NWFA.

(Over the Garden Wall)
Over The Garden Wall - 1959
5400ft. 60mins. Cert U (uncut)
Evans Above – 20th July 1959
1380ft. Cert U (with cuts)
Archive Status: Held at the NWFA.

(Let's Have a Murder)
Stick 'em Up – 20th July 1959
4500ft. 49mins. Cert U (uncut)
Archive Status: Held at the NWFA.
(It's a Grand Life)
As You Were – 31st May 1960
1700ft. 18mins. Cert U (uncut)
Archive Status: Held at the NWFA.

(Unknown)
Threepenny Ballet – 30th November 1959
16mins.Cert U (uncut)
Archive Status: Lost.

The following are short circus subjects extracted from 'International
Circus Review'.

Visit to the Zoo – 22nd October 1956
709ft. Cert U (with cuts).

Circus Parade – 22nd October1956
1295ft. Cert U (uncut).

Pride of the Ring – 22ⁿᵈ October 1956
1397ft. Cert U (uncut)

The Big Show – 5ᵗʰ February 1959
1674ft. Cert U (uncut).

Zootime – 4ᵗʰ May 1961
809ft. Cert U (uncut).

Archive Status: All held at the NWFA.

A selection of films distributed by Planet Film Distributors

Most of the following are second feature/B movies or foreign language dubbed/subtitled films. A note of interest came from Mike Blakeley when he recalled how his father and Bill Chalmers had been offered the distribution rights to a series of foreign made Western films. Having viewed the first of these, Bill Chalmers decided he didn't like it and consequently turned down the rights to '*A Fistful of Dollars*' and the subsequent sequels. Belatedly playing catch-up Planet distributed '*The Tramplers*' and '*Treasure of Silver Lake*' both being Italian co-production Westerns

A Man Named John – 1967
Carasella - 1969
Cervantes - 1968
Chimes at Midnight -1967
City of Fear - 1966
Crazy Days (46mins) - 1962
Dutchman - 1967
Four Keys - 1967
Hercules and the Masked Rider - 1965
House of a Thousand Dolls - 1967
Indian Paint - 1965
Journey into Nowhere – 1962
Killers are Challenged - 1968
Kimberley Jim - 1966
One Week with Love - 1962
The Pawnbroker (Rod Steiger) - 1965
Sanders – 1965

Shadows of Tiran - 1968
Silent Invasion – 1961
The Tender Age - 1969
The Tramplers - 1967
Treasure of Silver Lake – 1964

Non-Blakeley Films of Interest

The first two films both star Frank Randle and are often mistaken for being Mancunian/Blakeley productions. The last film was produced at Film Studios Manchester.

Somewhere in Civvies - 1943
Offered to the BBFC for classification at a running time of 87m 43s
The classification of 'U' granted on 30th July was achieved with no cuts to the film
Production Company: Butchers Films (and Distribution)
Producer: T.A. Welsh
Director: Maclean Rogers
Story: Con West
Cinematographer: Geoffrey Faithfull
Cast Joss Ambler, Grey Blake, George Donnan, H.F. Maltby, Nancy O'Neil, Frank Randle, Suzette Tarri

When You Come Home - 1947
Offered to the BBFC for classification at a running time of 93m 23s
The classification of 'U' granted on 5th March was achieved with no cuts to the film
Production Company: F.W. Baker-Butcher.
Distribution: Butchers Film Services.
Film Studio: Nettlefold – Walton-on-Thames
Producer: John Baxter
Director: John Baxter
Screenplay: Geoffrey Orme, David Evans
Additional Scenes & Comedy Dialogue: Frank Randle
Cinematographer: Geoffrey Faithfull
Art Director: C. H. Gilbert
Editor: Ted Richards
Production Manager: E. S. Laurie
Assistant Director: Don Weeks
Musical Director: Percival Mackey

Camera: Arthur Grant
Continuity: Marion Ward
Make-up: Harry Webber
Original Songs, Written, Composed and Sung by: Leslie Sarony &
Leslie Holmes
Choreography: Fred Conyngham, Hazel Gee
CAST; Frank Randle, Leslie Sarony & Leslie Holmes, Diana Decker,
Fred Conyngham, Linda Parker, Jack Melford, Tony Heaton, Hilda
Bayley, Lily Lapidus, Lesley Osmond, Gus Aubrey, Ernest Dale,

Never Look Back - 1951
Offered to the BBFC for classification at a running time of 70m 41s
The classification of 'A' granted on 21ˢᵗ November was achieved with
no cuts to the film
Released 26ᵗʰ May 1952
Production Company: Hammer Film Productions Limited
Distribution: Exclusive Films Ltd
Studio: Film Studios Manchester
Sound System: Gaumont
Producer: Michael Carreras, James Brennan
Director: Francis Searle
Screenplay: John Hunter, Guy Morgan, Francis Searle
Cinematographer: Reginald Wyer
Assistant Producer: Thomas Blakeley
Assistant Director: Pat Kelly
Music: Temple Abady
Editor: John Ferris
Art Director: Alec Gray
Camera: Ken Hodges
Sound: Sid Wiles
Continuity: Connie Willis
Make-up: Peter Evans
Hair Stylist: Monica Hustler
Wardrobe: Molly Arbuthnot
Casting Director: Nora Roberts
Music Performed by the Philharmonia Orchestra
Production Manager: Anthony Nelson Keys
Cast: Rosamund John, Hugh Sinclair, Guy Middleton, Henry
Edwards, Terence Longdon, John Warwick, Brenda de Banzie, Arthur
Howard, H.S. Hills, Bruce Belfrage, Helene Burls, Frances Rowe, Bill
Shine, Barbara Shaw, David Scase, Norman Somers, June Mitchell